More Praise for *Peer-to-Peer Leadership*

"Baker captures exactly what we all see happening in organizations. The power of relationships enables positive change regardless of existing systems, processes, and hierarchy. Baker has a keen eye for spotting these trends, investigating the data, and drawing cogent insights."
—**Joanna B. Miller, cofounder, Miller Black Associates, LLC**

"Baker captures powerful forces overlooked by old-school leadership and management models. Dismiss them at your peril!"
—**Christopher Whitfield, CEO, Batswadi Pharmaceuticals**

"Mila Baker challenges us to rethink all of our basic assumptions about how business enterprises are managed. She very convincingly argues that the hierarchical structure of leadership and management that characterized organizations in the Industrial Age not only has lost its relevance in today's world but might actually be a hindrance and a handicap. Be prepared to unlearn the conventional wisdom of a bygone era."
—**Emmy Miller, President, Liberty Business Strategies, Ltd.**

"Mila Baker challenges traditional modes of leadership in all institutional and organizational settings—corporate, civic, religious, and political. Technology now brings information at the same time to all participants in an enterprise. Therefore, the leader's role must shift—he or she must now manage the process of bringing shared information into the decision-making center and collectively arriving at a course of action where all participants have shared responsibility for outcomes. This book is indeed revolutionary."
—**Enith Williams, international business consultant and Member, World Ladies Group**

"*Peer-to-Peer Leadership* may make for uncomfortable reading in organizations reliant on hierarchy. Mila Baker describes and ably exemplifies an organizational peer-to-peer archetype requiring fundamental changes to organizations: to their leadership and their design. Thought provoking—the debate the book is sure to raise is exactly what a peer-to-peer organization would want to start to remodel itself."
—**Patricia Cichocki, founder, Design to Change, and coauthor of *Organization Design***

"Mila Baker's new peer-to-peer model of leadership is designed from the viewpoint that individuals are autonomous, collaborative, self-reliant, and able and willing to deal with changing circumstances to forward the purpose of their organization. Treat everyone as a leader and the organization will strengthen and grow—Baker's book shows how."
—**Peter Roche, cofounder and Managing Pai**

"Mila Baker really nails it in *Peer-to-Peer Le* can unleash the power in their organizatio freely. This book may make some leaders u ceed in the 21st century will embrace its cut

—**Bud Bilanich, "The Common Sense Guy," author and career mentor**

"The paradigm for effective leadership is changing. Companies can no longer rely on single individuals. And teams are not always best suited to address every situation. Fortunately, Mila Baker offers both practical and provocative insights leaders and followers alike can use to lead in an era of globalization, proliferating technology, and nonstop dialogue with customers—what she calls the 'peer-to-peer approach.'"
—**Claudy Jules, Global Lead, Human Capital Strategy, Accenture**

"Are you ready to rethink your notions of leadership and organization design? In this thought-provoking book, Mila Baker gets us to examine the way organizations really function and the way leadership works in a world where collaboration is king. Using examples from politics, business, computing, and education, Mila helps you explore what it means to be a leader and a follower in a networked world. Read this book from cover to cover; you will be glad you did."
—**Dick and Emily Axelrod, authors of the forthcoming *Time Well Spent***

"Equipotency. Take a good look at that word. P2P architecture, as well as your future and mine, is built upon it. Equipotency, node communities, and the 'new' relational dynamics you'll learn about in this book aren't theory. Far from it. They're here *now*. Box up the old gadgets before it's too late. What an amazing book! I can't wait to buy a full case to share."
—**David Sanford, author, speaker, consultant, and Director of Institutional Marketing, Corban University**

"Mila Baker has conceived a powerful 21st-century model of human organization. Of particular interest is the fluidity of leading and following when team members work in 'equipotent,' nonhierarchical relationships. She helps us see and understand the evolution that is occurring in our lifetime and how to harness its full potential."
—**Ira Chaleff, author of *The Courageous Follower***

"A revolution in the concept of leadership is afoot. Baker's paradigm-shattering insight into the nature of peer networking redefines the whole field of leadership studies by illustrating that modern leadership is a characteristic of groups that function more like a peer-to-peer computer network than a command-and-control hierarchy."
—**Tom Thomson, Adjunct Professor, New York University**

"Applying lessons learned from technology and social media, Mila Baker's *Peer-to-Peer Leadership* breaks new ground in presenting how peer-to-peer interactions can fundamentally change organizations. A must-read."
—**Frederick A. Miller, CEO, and Judith H. Katz, Executive Vice President, The Kaleel Jamison Consulting Group, Inc., and coauthors of *The Inclusion Breakthrough* and *Opening Doors to Teamwork and Collaboration***

PEER
TO
PEER
LEADERSHIP

WHY THE NETWORK
IS THE LEADER

Mila N. Baker

BK

Berrett–Koehler Publishers, Inc.
San Francisco
a BK Business book

Berrett-Koehler Publishers, Inc.

235 Montgomery Street, Suite 650

San Francisco, CA 94104-2916

Tel: (415) 288-0260   Fax: (415) 362-2512   www.bkconnection.com

Ordering Information
Quantity sales. Special discounts are available on quantity purchases by corporations, associations, and others. For details, contact the "Special Sales Department" at the Berrett-Koehler address above.

Individual sales. Berrett-Koehler publications are available through most bookstores. They can also be ordered directly from Berrett-Koehler: Tel: (800) 929-2929; Fax: (802) 864-7626; www.bkconnection.com

Orders for college textbook/course adoption use. Please contact Berrett-Koehler: Tel: (800) 929-2929; Fax: (802) 864-7626.

Orders by U.S. trade bookstores and wholesalers. Please contact Ingram Publisher Services, Tel: (800) 509-4887; Fax: (800) 838-1149; E-mail: customer.service@ingrampublisherservices.com; or visit www.ingrampublisherservices.com/Ordering for details about electronic ordering.

Berrett-Koehler and the BK logo are registered trademarks of Berrett-Koehler Publishers, Inc.

Printed in the United States of America

Berrett-Koehler books are printed on long-lasting acid-free paper. When it is available, we choose paper that has been manufactured by environmentally responsible processes. These may include using trees grown in sustainable forests, incorporating recycled paper, minimizing chlorine in bleaching, or recycling the energy produced at the paper mill.

Library of Congress Cataloging-in-Publication Data
Baker, Mila.
  Peer-to-peer leadership : why the network is the leader / Mila Baker.
-- First edition.
    pages cm
  Summary: "From a top scholar and corporate executive comes a new vision for leadership; the days of top down management are numbered, but the potential for peer-to-peer leadership is limitless"-- Provided by publisher.
  Includes bibliographical references and index.
  ISBN 978-1-60994-747-7 (pbk.)
  1. Leadership. 2. Organizational change. 3. Organizational behavior. 4. Peer-to-peer architecture (Computer networks)--Social aspects. 5. Business networks. 6. System theory. I. Title.
  HD57.7.B3473 2014
  658.4'092--dc23
                        2013036469
First Edition

18 17 16 15 14   10 9 8 7 6 5 4 3 2 1

Project Management: Lisa Crowder; Adept Content Solutions; Urbana, IL

Full-service book production: Adept Content Solutions; Urbana, IL

Cover Design: Permastudio

Author Photo: © NYU-SCPS/Mark McQueen

for Chista Mela Baker

OPPORTUNITY

The leader enters the door each day.
The follower enters the door each day.
Both enter the door to serve.
The leader serves the organization.
The follower serves the leader.
Each day an opportunity is lost.

Contents

Figures and Examples

Preface

The journey to write this book started as I completed work on a major merger project assignment at one of the largest pharmaceutical companies in the world. After going through phases of personal leadership and experiencing the continued futility of trying to fit our existing leadership theories, models, and language into a new world reality, it became clear to me what people mean when they say insanity is doing the same things over and over and expecting different results. This became clear in three phases of my learning curve about leadership: invisible leadership, leadership theory shopping, and bold, new ways of thinking about leadership and organization design— leadership through community.

The invisible leadership phase started with my first experience as a new manager and leader. I recognized that as a newly minted PhD I had a lot of theoretical knowledge, but little practical knowledge and experience. I wanted to apply the knowledge I had learned in graduate school, but I also wanted to experiment with and test new ideas. I wanted to let others learn how to achieve results and personal success on their own. There were many people I worked with who were more experienced than I was, and while I wanted to learn from them, I didn't necessarily want to follow exactly in their footsteps.

I focused on asking others what they thought before I expressed my point of view or perspective. I quickly learned that some individuals who reported to me were uncomfortable with being asked their thoughts. They were confused, looked for me to provide more direction, and perceived their jobs as solely following orders and doing what the manager wanted them to do. Others expressed different points of view, and I was tentative and unclear in my response. It was not until months later that one person on my staff told me how uncomfortable everyone was with being asked their thoughts; no manager had ever asked them what they thought, and they were intimidated when asked to share their thoughts because they were afraid they would not say what I wanted.

At the same time, my manager did not think I was taking control as a manager and thought that I relied too heavily on consensus of the group. He wanted me to be direct and tell those working for me what he wanted and what he had directed us to do. Demonstrating through my actions how I expected my reports to behave and make decisions turned out to be too subtle an approach and did not provide enough guidance and direction. It did not take long to realize that invisible and silent leadership translated as no leadership to many.

From the invisible leadership phase, I moved to a phase of leadership theory shopping—a phase where I tried on different leadership styles to see what seemed to work best in different contexts or situations. As an academic, I was well versed in all the current theories and regularly tried most of them to see how others would respond. I tried to absorb and use not only the leadership theories I had been introduced to as a doctoral student, but also all the new theories that arrived on bookshelves daily. Keeping up with new trends and practices felt like taking an intense crash course every few months. Every conference, seminar, and expert lecture I attended added more material to an already overloaded brain repository of leadership information.

I quickly learned that some theories were considerably better than others, but while each approach yielded some success, there was always some aspect that resulted in unintended consequences (or completely failed to deliver the expected results). After many interventions and attempts to apply theoretical approaches, it was clear that adding yet another new approach to the existing toolbox was not the answer.

Soon after I completed work on the major merger assignment at one of the largest pharmaceutical companies in the world, I realized it had been a tremendous two-year learning experience. It opened my eyes to the strength and importance of change, transformation, and leadership. It also humbled me. For the first time, I was acutely aware of how important a leader's work can be for the lives and livelihood of many people, let alone an organization as a whole. Going forward, I felt it my professional duty, moral obligation, and ethical responsibility to do whatever I could to ensure the organizations with which I worked had the guidance, advice, and support needed to ensure more positive outcomes that would enhance organizational performance as well as the quality of life for all those along the chain of command. I realized I was beginning to make the transition from scholar-practitioner to practitioner-scholar. This was an important distinction for me, and helped me realize that my practice—my daily work—would be more formative than what I read in new books and journal articles. I realized that the act of doing the work was very powerful and significantly influenced my thinking about the work. I was beginning to form my interpretation of what leadership should be.

A brief period of reflection followed my work on the
pharmaceutical companies' merger. This pause allowed me
to recognize that something else was needed, not only in
the way I worked, but also in the way I helped others. The
status quo was no longer sufficient, and neither were the
theoretical models currently in use. In one sense, it was
somewhat disturbing that I had not appreciated the value
of deep reflection before, since that is a core of the work of a
practitioner and scholar of strategic change and leadership.
But I was gratified and energized that I was now embarking
on a period of reflection that would lead to a new level of
thought and introspection on the work I was so passionate
about. I felt confident that it would inform and direct me
going forward—that it would become the footprint for the
next phase of my professional life.

Fueled by the merger experience (and a re-reading
of Meg Wheatley's bestselling book, *Leadership and the
New Science*), I began a journey to explore a bold, new
paradigm for leadership and organizational design. I never
thought that the theories in use were useless and should be
discarded. On the contrary, I thought about them in terms of
the fairy tale of the emperor and his clothes. In this instance,
it was not that the emperor was not wearing any clothes so
much as that he had an outdated wardrobe—a somewhat
restrictive wardrobe not suited for the conditions of the
twenty-first century.

Seeing the emperor dressed so poorly, I saw the need
to figure out what type of wardrobe best suits leaders
and organizations in the twenty-first century. Rather
than construct new architectural forms and structures,
my approach was to look for ways to create form and
structure from natural order—similar to Frank Lloyd
Wright's architectural approach. I wanted to explore ways

consistent with natural order and chaos. I did not want to impress one more theory upon the natural order of the time, but hoped to harness some of the power inherent in that order. For our time, that order is the architecture of the peer-to-peer network.

About This Book

This book uses the analogy of peer-to-peer information technology architecture to demonstrate how technological advances can help guide our thinking about a new paradigm for leadership and organizational design. It does not view technology as a barrier or a threat, but rather sees it as an enabler of greater understanding about the integral connections between individuals in organizations and how work can be organized for optimal success. It introduces a new way to define, measure, and express leadership in a world that is now hyper-digitally connected and brings the challenges that prevent us from altering the way we think about leadership to the surface.

Peer to peer (P2P) IT architecture is a radical, architectural shift that has transformed the computing industry and influenced how society uses computer technology. Beyond that, it has ignited an interest in examining many social peer-to-peer processes and relationships where interaction—especially in large organizations—traditionally occurs in accordance with the model of command-and-control leadership. With P2P, it becomes possible for leaders to relinquish some of that command and control, and for individuals to be equals.

The book itself is organized around two important concepts—leadership and organization design. There are three elements and patterns: (1) node communities,

(2) equipotency, and (3) relational dynamics. Like the colors and patterns in a kaleidoscope, these themes weave a new tapestry for leadership and for organization design. Their interplay forms a somewhat abstract but integrated look at the whole organization.

While the first chapter takes a look at the current state of leadership, the language of leadership, and the language of the peer-to-peer architecture (P2P), chapters two through four each deal with a particularly important piece of P2P architecture: *nodes and node communities, equipotency,* and *relational dynamics,* respectively. Chapters five through eight provide guidance and background for understanding the importance of and need for a fundamental shift, as well as examples of people and organizations that have put P2P leadership and organizational structure into practice. Chapters nine and ten outline the P2P implications for leadership, for organization design, and for how P2P can be practiced in the twenty-first-century organization. I talk about how decisions in organizations are influenced by their leadership practices and their organizational design, about possibilities and a vision for the future of leadership, and about the mindset, perspective, and behaviors needed to realize a new vision. The book also highlights a few companies that are already on the P2P path and authors who are outlining new behaviors consistent with P2P network communities. In addition to presenting ideas, the book provides examples of what we could do differently to build momentum toward the vision of P2P leadership. To that end, the book is more about ideas than practices and frameworks. It is an invitation for you to put yourself in a new scenario and a new reality—one that is almost undeniably imminent, whether our organizations are ready for it or not. It is intended to provoke thought, spark questions, and conjure images of possibilities that can be tested and tried in the arenas of leadership and organizational design.

This book is for doers, thinkers, and helpers. It is for those who must take action, those who enjoy thinking and inquiry, and those who are committed to helping others. It is not for pessimists, for those who are comfortable with the outcomes of current practices, or for those who think the state of leadership is well and will continue to flourish as it is. Regardless of organizational position or status, it is for and will benefit those who think and feel passionately that we can and must improve the quality of leadership actions, research, teaching, and consulting, as well as the overall design of organizations and leadership programs.

The book is not a review of theories or a book of facts. It is not a scholarly treatise on leadership. Rather, it is a journey on a new road—a road not taken before. There is a quote carved on a bench in front of my children's upper school that reads: "I believe in the sun even when it rains." To this day, this quote is the first that comes to mind when I think about moving forward by embracing the opportunity presented at the moment. In that spirit, I invite you to join me on a new road.

Mila N. Baker
New York, New York
October, 2013

1
The
Language
of Leadership

The current definitions and historical models of leadership are rooted in the relationship between two entities—leader and follower. Terms such as "leader-member," "in-group and out-group," "power over," talent and workforce, and "power through" highlight the traditional models, while terms such as "empowerment," "subordinates," and "followers" conjure up images of servitude and second-class citizenship. All of them differentiate each entity in terms of status and imply a certain level of inequality. There is no job description for or position called "Follower Specialist." The role of follower is more often than not viewed in negative terms while the role of leader represents a virtuous mantle of aspiration. Leadership was, and largely still is, reserved for a very few while the very many follow. The language of leadership reflects and supports this division between leader and follower, and neither the definition nor the language of leadership is sufficient for the world today.

After the Great Depression of the 1930s in the United States and the post-World War II era when people returned to work, loyal followership often guaranteed lifelong employment and ensured that one could care for and feed one's family (and, upon retirement, get a watch as a token of appreciation). Employers could almost guarantee that subordinates would do whatever was necessary to earn their pay and small rewards. The negative connotation of the word "follower" was far less painful to swallow than the inability to care for oneself or one's family. Even as the informal and unwritten employment contracts began to erode and change in the latter part of the twentieth century, only to be rendered completely obsolete in the twenty-first century, there were many instances where employees felt compelled to follow blindly—even in situations of blatant abuse and illegal behavior. The economic conditions of the time helped support the divide and distinctions between leaders and followers. The landscape has changed quite a bit since the 1930s, but the language we use remains a remnant of a bygone past. Our responses to and the visceral images created by that language linger. Instead of reinforcing age-old divisions, we need a mindset and language of leadership that maintains equilibrium between leading and following—a conception of leadership that is agile and stateless in its composition. Like the U.S. constitution guides and influences the nation's trajectory without stifling the rights and freedoms of its populace, organizations' designs need to facilitate leading and following on an equal platform. Neither leaders nor followers can achieve success without the other, and both can render an organization non-competitive or cause it to underachieve its mission.

Leadership and the Tech Revolution

The rapid advancement of technology and the proliferation of mobile and other network-attached devices have been the catalyst and tipping point for all types of changes in how we consume media, organize data, and communicate with each other. The medium and the messages are shifting. Conversely, our views of leadership and organizational life have been slow to change. These fundamental shifts in technology and media consumption have blurred the boundaries of communication within organizations, which has in turn blurred the distinction between leaders and followers and also the media and messages they use to communicate. Traditional leadership models and prevailing paradigms based on these roles are no longer suited for the world we live in today. A digital revolution is driving complexity and pace. It presents enormous challenge and opportunity. There are new computational tools and voluminous data of all types.

One of the most profound shifts has been an erosion of individual power and authority, with an unearthing of collective power enabled through social media. Historically, power and authority have been granted to or taken by a few and reinforced through organizational hierarchy and structure. Today, informal, social networks like Twitter and Facebook are usurping the power of some formal, hierarchical networks. We need to challenge ourselves and ask the question, What is the rationale for maintaining the outmoded and cumbersome organizational layers and vertical hierarchies? Why haven't we embraced Fritz Capra's notion that all learning systems are coordinated by network? We have been discussing the notion of the organization as a social system for quite some time.

While the focus on informal networks is generally discussed in terms of social networks and social relationships—not related to power and authority within networks—each of these shifts challenges the notion of command-and-control leadership and the clearly delineated roles of leader and follower. In the case of the Arab Spring, informal networks allowed individuals to organize more efficiently. The power of subordinates and followers was significantly elevated, and traditional, hierarchical leadership was overthrown in a very concrete way.

Technology has also disrupted structural boundaries within organizations. Like an earthquake fault line that releases energy associated with rapid movement and structural shifting, there is a leadership fault line that has fractured and resulted in discontinuity and a permanent fracture in our traditional leadership formations. The organization is flattened, matrixed, and decentralized as it incorporates tools and emerging technologies into many areas of operation (e.g., enterprise systems, social media for customers and potential employees, etc.). The structural boundaries within organizations have been permanently altered as a result of technological eruptions and explosions and to accommodate some of the shifts, leaders and followers move into these new forms of organizational structure.

Too often, organizations see technological advances as, primarily, the Information Technology department's responsibility. External forces, customer demands, or security concerns often drive how an organization responds to shifts in landscape, be they technological or otherwise. Organizations rarely integrate internal organizational changes in advance of a specific cause-and-effect event. This lack of planning places an organization in a perpetual cycle of reactionary change and, frequently, behind the curve. Rather than temper or hedge the effect of technology on an organization's infrastructure, the desired action should be to embrace new developments and leverage them to their fullest potential.

The shift to power of the masses within organizations is unleashing the grip of command-and-control leadership. More specifically, command-and-control leadership is losing its grip on the organizational clutch. Where hierarchy and traditional organizational structures either intentionally or unintentionally acted as a barrier to equality, new technological advances erase those barriers. Even when leaders within traditional models make attempts to treat everyone as an equal and genuinely see the value of doing so, the traditional organizational structures and lexicon stand as impermeable, and often invisible, barriers. Leading in the twenty-first century requires a new structure and design that is more suited to the realities of today. This is a journey that many organizations have begun, and they are taking steps forward.

Individuality and Equality

In recent years, there has been a shift in the balance between organizational leadership and individuality evidenced by the disparity between pay among senior leaders and pay for the average worker. The justification for the increase in CEO compensation and the huge severance packages for senior executives who leave underperforming organizations are reflections of the focus on the value of the individual.

Since the founding of the United States, the balance between individuality and equality has, over time, shifted toward one pole or the other. Where power was once concentrated in the hands of few at the top of traditional hierarchies, the revolutions in technology have abruptly swung the pendulum back toward equality of the masses. The influence of power and authority has diminished.

Today, new books have surfaced that discuss the rise of the power of followers, the need for more empowerment, or how to make leaders act like followers and followers act like leaders. There have been calls to de-emphasize command-and-control leadership in favor of a more matrixed or hybrid organization structure. In spite of all the adjustments—command-and-control tweaks and redesign, ultimately—the language and message is still rooted in a model dominated by traditional hierarchy.

What Is Peer-to-Peer Computing Technology and How Is It Related to Leadership?

Today, computer technology is no longer just a tool, but a social and structural phenomenon that makes information readily accessible and more transparent. In an environment where communication comes in real time and from closer to the source (if not the source itself), anyone can take the lead. In its classic sense, peer-to-peer (P2P) computing is network architecture for data sharing. Its use began more than thirty years ago and moved onto the center stage of computing with the introduction of distributed music file sharing at the turn of the twenty-first century. For our purposes, peer-to-peer is a type of architecture that influences the transfer of information, social exchange, and discourse.

The P2P architecture is unique in that its processes are built using dynamic and changing structures that adapt themselves as needed. Where older, client-server systems required information to be centralized and then distributed from that center, the dynamic structures within P2P comprise a network of peer *nodes* (computers, phones, and other devices) used for communication and collaboration. Information is decentralized, and all nodes can send and receive information within a P2P network. The interaction or exchange between peer nodes is a relational dynamic that reflects an egalitarian network. All nodes within a P2P network are equal and function as equally privileged participants in the larger whole—a concept known as *equipotency*.

Equipotency is based on an operational premise that the P2P network does not know where a needed resource

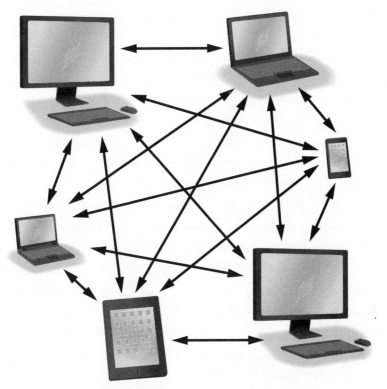

Figure 1: Peer to peer IT architecture

or asset will be located, and that any node may be capable
of being a resource to any other node in that network. The
architectural structure is designed so that every available
node can be ready to fulfill a need as it arises. In their dual
roles, all peer nodes are both suppliers and consumers of
resources (assets). Each node supplies or shares assets and
each node consumes resources based on need.

In traditional, client-server models, formal rules dictate
the role of client and the role of server—information flows
from the centralized server out to the client. The P2P
architecture is a departure from the traditional client-server
model in that there are no formal rules or advance decisions
made to determine whom the participatory members
are or how they must relate to each other. All rules are
generated from within, and there is no central coordinator
or dedicated master server.

The P2P model can be used to reframe the concept of
organizational leadership and organizational architecture.
It enables us to take a fresh new look at the authoritarian
and centralized notions of current organizational leadership
approaches. While traditional hierarchies place emphasis
on a certain chain of command, P2P architecture places
emphasis on the organizing and indexing of data (both
archival, real-time inputs), so that nodes in the organization
act as both servers and clients (senders and receivers) of the
data. In this model, the network itself becomes the leader as
it constantly computes raw data and turns it into actionable
information.

In a P2P organization, layers are flattened, and spans
are spherical. Each node is interdependent on the next,
making each node responsible and accountable to the
whole and allowing the question of what should be done
to supersede the question of who is in charge. Cooperation

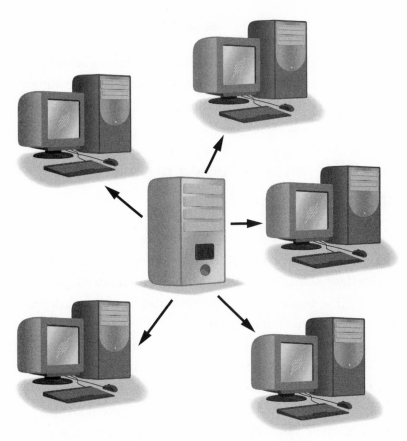

Figure 2: Client server model

and collaboration among and between equals to achieve common tasks in pursuit of a common good then becomes far more important than an individual's traditional status as a "leader" or "follower."

The Difference between a New Theory and a Paradigm Shift

Traditional organizational structures are based on mechanical models of organizations from the Frederick Taylor days of industrial management and leadership. As late as the 1960s, the literature surrounding organizational structure described it using mechanical language—cogs on a wheel. While the mechanical command-and-control leadership models are still alive and thriving, technology has forced us to confront a new reality—organization structures cannot be understood in purely mechanical terms. There is a natural order to the flow and structure within an organization that now calls for correction and a fundamental shift in the understanding of leadership. It is a shift to a model where knowledge and intelligence is distributed throughout the organization from the periphery of the system to the center of the system—a shift that allows us to look at a more integrative model between individuals, work units, and the organization. Rather than seeing each as separate, mechanical entities or organizational silos, the shift to P2P allows us to see combinations of natural, organizing entities.

Those of us who practice or teach leadership have lulled ourselves into a false sense of security with the proliferation of new theories and new books on leadership, but these theories are largely remiss in detailing the fundamental change in landscape sculpted by the rise of informal networks. This failure to see the P2P future threatens to push organizations who embrace traditional leadership structures into a reactionary corner rather than a position of being able to leverage the powers of this new, natural order.

As early as 1935, Kurt Lewin wrote of the importance of the interactions between individuals and their environment.[1] More recently, Ira Chaleff spoke of the shift in the balance of power between leaders and followers and how leaders can no longer ignore the influence of internal and external stakeholders.[2] There is now recognition that broader context and all constituents are critical—not just customers, employees, and shareholders; not just founders and donors.

Informal networks have become as powerful as traditional hierarchies—and in some cases, more powerful. Organizations have responded in a variety of ways that range from putting constraints on employees' use of services like Facebook and Twitter to doing nothing at all. In attempts to bring parity between leaders and followers, organizations are beginning to recognize this as a futile effort given the current structure of organizations and many governments, but few if any have tried to harness the power of peer-to-peer architecture in the very structure of their organizations.

In most organizations, relationships and information flow are organized in some form of hierarchical structure, but this doesn't need to be the only model. From popular movements in Tunisia and Egypt to Occupy Wall Street (OWS), the influence of an integrated network of equally privileged participants sharing information is producing a radical paradigm shift in the way we connect and relate to one another. People in social networks act much like "peer nodes" in P2P network architecture. The world no longer must rely on traditional hierarchical order to transmit or receive information.

Summary

When Canadian geese migrate, they fly in a V-formation to move quickly and fly longer than they could as individuals. Geese use synergy—the law of nature that recognizes that working together creates a greater result than could be achieved alone. The pendulum has swung such that leadership now requires synergy and an adjustment that better suits the realities of the time. The rationale for the importance of both leading and following is that data moves too quickly. No one has the capacity to know everything they need to know or to convert all the data to information needed to be successful in the twenty-first century.

What we have is not working. The disparity between principle and established practice is transparent to the masses. Elaborate leadership development programs, coaching initiatives, a proliferation of leadership books and "best practice" guidance, and reinforcement from other organizations that only expand on current practice are no longer viable solutions or sufficient for building effective leadership. Barbara Kellerman, a Harvard professor, leadership expert, and author of *The End of Leadership*[3] has questioned whether the leadership industry—with its myriad of books, articles and training— actually does what it claims to do: that is, grow leaders. She also questions whether leadership can be taught at all. Its demands have certainly shifted. Few organizations have adjusted or adapted to the new reality, and still fewer see the integral connection between organizational leadership and organization design. Informal networks like Facebook and Twitter are becoming more powerful than many organizational structures, and current leadership approaches and organization designs are not aligned to the new reality. To the contrary, we have seen more transparency to failed leadership and more calls for a new approach.

Leadership in today's world requires insight from more than one individual. We must rely constantly on others' insight even when we are in a position of authority. In the coming chapters, we'll look at the power inherent in P2P architecture for organizational design, organizational structure, and leadership.

Practical Application

Jot down all the things that you did this week that you would not (or could not) have done five years ago.

Key Points

▶ The current leadership lexicon is insufficient for today's world.

▶ The fundamental shifts in technology and media consumption have blurred the boundaries and eroded power and authority within organizations.

▶ The peer-to-peer (P2P) IT architecture model can be used to reframe the concept of organizational leadership and organizational architecture and design.

▶ The concepts of the node, node community, equipotency, and relational dynamics will frame a new concept of leadership more suited for the twenty-first century.

▶ The world no longer has to rely on traditional hierarchy to transmit information.

② Node Community

Big-screen televisions lined the bar at the Lucky Strike Bowling Alley overlooking the Hudson River in New York City. Comfortable chairs, couches, and cocktail tables invited non-bowling enthusiasts to enjoy their tête-à-tête without missing anything on the big screen. My family and several friends ordered our first round of drinks in anticipation of the first 2012 presidential debate between President Barack Obama and Mitt Romney, former governor of Massachusetts. As we settled in, commentator Jim Lehrer began his introduction to the media-hyped debate.

The debate started slowly, continuing at an uneventful pace and maintaining a blasé tone until Mr. Romney repeated a comment he had previously made about wanting to cut funding to the U.S. Public Broadcasting System (PBS). But this time, he added a new twist; if elected president, he would eliminate funding to the PBS and *fire* Big Bird!

Fire Big Bird? The kind, likeable, compassionate, and bigger-than-life yellow bird with the orange beak? The bird that has been an iconic American symbol for at least three generations—both in the United States and throughout the world?[4]

Almost instantly, Mr. Romney's quote was heard around the world. "What things would I cut from spending? Well, first of all, I will eliminate all programs by this test, if they don't pass it. Is the program so critical it's worth borrowing money from China to pay for it? And if not, I'll get rid of it. Obamacare's on my list. I apologize, Mr. President. I use that term with all respect, by the way. I'm sorry, Jim, I'm going to stop the subsidy to PBS. I'm going to stop other things. I like PBS, I love Big Bird. Actually I like you, too. But I'm not going to, I'm not going to keep on spending money on things to borrow money from China to pay for. That's number one."

As soon as Mr. Romney uttered his threat to cut PBS spending, everyone stared at the dozen or so television screens. The apathy and disinterest that was setting in from listening to a repetition of stump speech rhetoric from both candidates suddenly ignited and became fireworks of disbelief! Stares instantly shifted and people cried out loud in unison: "Big Bird! How could anyone say they want to fire Big Bird?! Why would anyone interject Big Bird into a political conversation?" A boring and—given the extraordinary media hype—disappointing debate shifted abruptly.

Within seconds, almost everyone in the bowling alley focused their attention on their mobile devices. They logged onto Facebook and Twitter, posting their amusement with, disbelief of, or support for, the potential unemployment of a well-loved character from our collective American childhood. Within minutes, there were hundreds of likes on comments from my son's high school friends: "Save Big Bird!" While the debate languished and the candidates lapsed into more boring, repetitive rhetoric, the social media community buzzed with energy. Thousands of Twitter and Facebook posts were simultaneously sent and received around the world. A community of Big Bird sympathizers formed—a Big Bird node community.

What Is a Node Community?

As mentioned in chapter one, a node is part of the taxonomy used in peer-to-peer (P2P) IT architecture. In this type of architecture, a node represents each computer in a network, and a node community represents every computer in the network. Unlike a client-server system, where there are two distinct entities in the computer network system (the server that selectively provides resources and the client

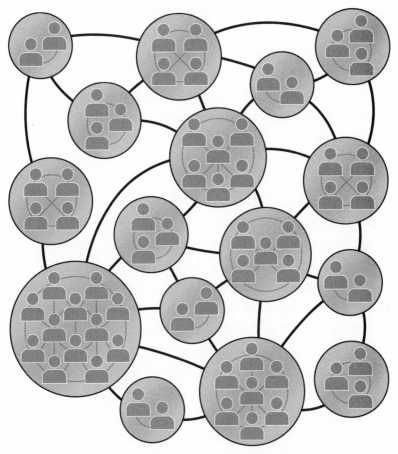

Figure 3: Peer to peer network community

that uses resources for their work), in peer-to-peer IT architecture, there is one primary entity: the node. Each node shares resources in order to do its work, and each node both provides and requests services. Each node is able to communicate directly, without passing through intermediaries.[5]

In a P2P organization network community, individuals represent nodes, and the node community is comprised of individuals working for a common purpose or toward a common result. In the response to Romney's Big Bird comment, each individual posting to social networks represented a node that was able to instantly connect with another node—another person or group—simply by sending or receiving information about firing Big Bird. Each node both shared information and received it. Some nodes were Big Bird sympathizers, some rallied behind Mr. Romney, and both were able to communicate their messages instantaneously, without any third party intervention.

Node communities formed within minutes of Romney's comment. They started spontaneously, originating from sympathizers upset at the perceived potential elimination of Big Bird. Each node was an individual connector in the larger community—a community where a plethora of connections and receptors could rapidly send messages and receive them in nanoseconds. They could send and receive information both within their immediate surroundings and across continents and around the world.

Within a node community, information is received by one node and is easily and quickly passed to another. As new nodes join, the community expands. Individuals and organizations now no longer have to rely on a central source for information as in a client-server network or the traditional hierarchy in organizations. Technology has enabled a new communication model and paradigm and has disrupted the traditional organization communication pattern and hierarchy. Where information once flowed from manager to subordinate, it now flows freely from peer to peer.

The Power of Node Communities: Instant Information Sharing

Within a week, the Big Bird Node Community had exponentially grown. The power was in the node community as evidenced by major newspapers picking up the story and following with lead stories, articles, and opinion editorials about the response.[6] Weekly magazines carried articles from many writers, and internet news sites like the *Huffington Post* weighed in on discussions. Gov. Romney's Big Bird comment became one of the campaign's pivotal points. Incredibly, the scale of a largely spontaneous reaction to a comment about a fictitious character was met with rapid return fire and incredulous astonishment! Mr. Romney and his campaign were forced to temper the outcry by attempting to explain his intent and redirect his comment over firing Big Bird.

The power of nodes and node communities is also evident in the influence of social media on customer service. In the past, individual cases were handled in a customer service complaint department. Supervisors handled tougher situations, but complaints rarely reached the attention of anyone above government middle management. News of mistreatment by a particular company hardly ever moved beyond an individual's immediate social circle.

Today, the landscape is dramatically different. Gone are the days when disgruntled customers had minimal impact on sales, stock prices, or the overall perception of an institution. A post to Facebook or a 140-character complaint on Twitter can have a profound effect on a company's bottom line performance, an organization's funding, or an academic institution's enrollment. For instance, a musician and United Airlines passenger named Dave Carroll once found that baggage handlers had destroyed his guitar during a flight. After the airline refused to replace the badly damaged instrument, Carroll penned a now infamous song—"United Breaks Guitars"—created a video, and posted it to peer-to-peer video sharing site YouTube. The video and song that skewered United's customer service has since garnered over 12 million views; some claim it even had an impact on United's stock prices.

Dave Carroll employed computer technology to disrupt and raise awareness of United Airlines' customer service practice; regardless of whether or not it had a substantial effect on United's bottom line, the impact of social technology to transfer information rapidly and influence formal structures and processes certainly reaches beyond the one encounter with a customer service representative. Computer technology is no longer just a tool; it is a social phenomenon that makes information readily accessible and more transparent. It makes reliable communication in real time possible. Anyone can take the lead.

Power to Create Change and the Dangers of Misinformation

A node community is a wonderful example of the extraordinary power of technology, where individual connectors (nodes) can instantaneously move information among themselves. Add to this speed the ability to improve and add value to the information while correcting inaccuracies as soon as they crop up and extending access to those who would not otherwise have the information in traditional hierarchies, and we have a whole new communication revolution capable of toppling the whims of a would-be leader, or anyone with the intent to withhold information. We don't have to look far for an example. As mentioned earlier, social media outlets and node communities fanned the flames of the Arab Spring uprisings that began in Tunisia in December 2010 and moved quickly to Egypt, Libya, Syria, Yemen, and other countries in the Middle East. This resulted in the removal of more than one leader.

At the other extreme, nodes can also pass along inaccurate, unwanted, or unintentional information in the same instant fashion. Take, for example, a sophomore at a large urban university who accidentally clicked "Reply To All" in forwarding a note to his mother that the university had sent to him, only to find the note went to every student at the university! Upon receiving this note, students recognized their power and began sending frivolous messages. This inadvertent consequence of the power that just one node community had within the university was not trivial.

Social media also spun out of control in a negative way when Ryan Lanza (older brother to Newtown, Massachusetts shooter Adam Lanza) was accidentally identified as the suspect in the Newtown shooting. Based on news networks identifying him as the shooter, Ryan Lanza was wrongfully maligned as a mass-murderer, and social networks like Facebook and Twitter were almost instantly alight with modern torches and pitchforks—people created myriad anti-Ryan Lanza groups based on inaccurate information that had been disseminated quickly.[7] Like any new and powerful technology, there is always a danger that tools will be misused. The more we are aware of potential dangers and challenges, the more likely we will be to anticipate and avoid them.

Disruption of Traditional Communication Models

When we think of disruptive technologies, we think of products like the digital camera, the iPod, and file-sharing services like Napster—which, legal issues aside, paved the way for a broader embrace of peer-to-peer architecture. But

ON THE P2P PATH
Giant Hydra

Named after a fictional multi-headed beast, Giant Hydra is a new company that provides a vehicle for ad agencies and advertisers to access a pool of talent from around the world. Rather than send out RFPs and require individuals to compete with one another, they bring talent together in a network community. Giant Hydra uses a mass collaboration model to bring talented individuals together to work on projects. They meet in virtual spaces and form a team to work toward a common outcome and purpose. They work together to bring their ideas and creativity to a problem. Their skills are mixed and matched depending upon the need. They work from anywhere, anytime.

http://www.gianthydra.com

nodes and node communities are more than just disruptive technology—they are *disruptive organizational structures.* Unlike their technological counterparts, they disrupt the artificial structure and boundaries within organizations, resulting in the rise of organic and natural structural innovation.

Similar to what unfolded as the Medici Effect,[8] an original peer-to-peer community, the basic form of communication from one person to another can now be replicated within a node community anytime, from any place, and in many ways—it is a disruptive structure that is shaping a new and more natural organization design. While the traditional hierarchical organization design and structures were thought to bring order to chaos, what is appearing with nodes and node communities is the shift from an artificially drawn organization design and structure of boxes and lines to a more natural order of design consistent with natural chaos. Again, this is reminiscent of what occurred with the Medici Effect, which lasted two hundred years from the disruptive structural influence of one family.

The Value of Nodes and Node Communities in Organizations

Traditional organizations and hierarchies are defined at least in part by the boundaries they create within and without, but that needn't necessarily be the case. Node communities have an opportunity to evolve by rearranging some of the core presuppositions of traditional organizations. These are just a few of the value propositions that nodes and node communities present for organizations when they are considered more than just disruptive.

Efficient and Effective Flow of Information

Imagine the unlimited possibilities within organizations if the node and node community were viewed as core structural elements. If the node and node community were seen as natural organizational design structures that enable and provide open flow of and access to resources as opposed to creating boundaries and barriers among individuals, the idea of a bottleneck would become almost obsolete. With node communities equipped with the capacity for each node to work with information flowing in the form of documents and words, less time is wasted waiting for orders, productivity increases as available nodes are recruited for tasks needing assistance, and the overall goals of the organization retain a more central focus. Nodes can push or pull, freely share, and accept information from others while not having to depend on a central source to fulfill work assignments.

The Expertise of the Whole Community

In his bestselling book, *The Tipping Point*, Malcolm Gladwell describes the Law of the Few in explaining Milgram's six degrees of separation.[9] Six degrees of separation does not mean everyone is linked to everyone else within six steps. It means a very small number of people are linked to everyone else in a few steps, while the rest of us are linked to the world through those special few.[10] The node community and its supporting technology allow us to understand and use this phenomenon to improve how we work in organizations and how we predict outcomes. If decisions could be made in a timely manner or errors corrected as soon as they were noticed, risks would be anticipated and addressed more expeditiously. Weak links in the community would be identified, repaired or replaced, and all nodes would possess the capability to perform each function effortlessly. We would no longer have to rely on a few specialized skills or designated functions but would be able to draw on an entire node community for their expertise and insights.

Nimbleness and Response to Change

If the node is the physical entity connecting and binding a community, then the node community is the primary entity in which nodes connect. It is more than a social network: it is a *workflow network*—the architectural and structural design of how work gets done. The strength of the organization shifts from the strength of the individual making decisions to the degree to which information can be organized and used as a tool to make informed decisions by the whole. The organization of information is the broadest concept for decision making.

Where the power of traditional hierarchy was in its static chain of command and its ability to set and maintain boundaries, the power of the node community is in its ability to be dynamic and to shift according to a set of principles that guide how information is sent, received and organized. Because of the structure of traditional organizations, relations largely have to do with the boundaries they themselves have created. In node communities, relations have to do with what is actually occurring here and now, allowing for a certain nimbleness of response to internal and external change to which larger, more traditional organizations may take months or years to respond. Additionally, the power of the node and its community means they have an abundance of information to share and receive, where each infusion (via sending and receiving) increases the strength of their connectedness.

Real-Time Feedback and Dialogue

Feedback is only important if it is relevant now. Feedback should be given in real time, focused on what is happening now, and given because it helps organizations make better and more accurate assessments and decisions for the company and the industry. Dialogue, telling stories, and sharing are types of feedback with lasting benefits. This type of feedback is important to convey the human aspect of data and improves the quality of information—it humanizes the information human and gives it context. Feedback also encourages others to pay close attention to what their constituents are doing and then find meaningful ways to convey that action.

A real-time feedback system facilitates a broader face-to-face scoring system. The node community constantly sends and receives information that can only strengthen node connective tissues; it's an organic system for knowing how everyone is doing. The integrated nature of the node community facilitates real-time feedback and dialogue that can provide critical transfer of knowledge.

Summary

Stories like the ones surrounding Mitt Romney's proposed firing of Big Bird and Dave Carroll's very public complaints about customer service at United Airlines serve to illustrate the speed with which information can be sent and received among members of a node community. Gone are the days when successful P2P architecture depended on the decisions made by a few at the top of a traditional hierarchy. Nodes, with their dual roles of sending and receiving information, can communicate directly with each other with no need for a centralized, third party intermediary.

While the wrongful smearing and threatening of Ryan Lanza serves as a warning of what can go wrong with P2P architecture, there are numerous benefits and value propositions when the power of the network is harnessed for organizational design. The lack of a central authority figure enables the immediate flow of information between nodes and allows a network to adapt to new landscapes and scenarios more nimbly than organizations with rigid structures and boundaries. The type and number of connections within a node community also allows the skills and knowledge of the entire community to be leveraged and lets real-time feedback and dialogue occur; these are important elements in the overall growth and strengthening of an organization.

Practical Application

Think about a time when you have been a node. What was the situation? What was your role? What was the outcome? Was it positive or negative?

Key Points

▶ Where information used to flow from manager to subordinate, it now flows from peer to peer.

▶ Computer technology is no longer just a tool; it is also an enabler of organizational and social discourse.

▶ The Medici Effect was an early P2P node community.

▶ The dangers of the P2P network mirror some of its benefits—the speedy dissemination of information can also quickly spread misinformation.

▶ Node communities can rearrange some of the presuppositions of traditional organizations and provide great value to the organization.

③

Organizational
Equipotency

On December 3, 1979, the rock band The Who was scheduled to play a concert at 8 p.m. at Cincinnati Coliseum in Cincinnati, Ohio. By 6 p.m., masses of people had gathered outside the doors and were anxiously waiting to enter. When coliseum officials opened just a limited number of the many stadium entrances at 7:30 p.m., thousands of excited fans rushed in through the few doors simultaneously.

Some blocks away at the Cincinnati General Hospital emergency room, I was working the night shift in the psychiatric emergency room and was the shift lead. What began as a relatively calm night changed abruptly when groups of panicked, screaming people showed up at the ER—frantically begging for information about friends, children, and loved ones—asking things like "Are they alive?" and "Where can I find them?" For a few minutes, the emergency room staff had no idea that a riot had occurred not far from the hospital itself, but it was not long before someone volunteered information that drug users had stampeded the stadium and trampled eleven to death. The trampling accounts were quickly debunked as rumors.

Even without direct knowledge of the riot, the emergency room staff was swift and calm in their interactions with each person we encountered. Staff members stepped into whatever role needed to be filled in the moment. While one person went to the general ER to gather information about the situation, another alerted on-call staff that they would likely be needed. We attempted to reach hospital security and the Cincinnati police department to determine what to expect in the coming hours. We anticipated what preparations would be needed and moved swiftly. We remained calm, were alert to updated news, and were attentive to those seeking information. In short, everyone on duty did what was needed when it needed to be done. We knew our standard operating procedures, how to take care of those who presented at the ER doors, how to maintain a professional manner under stress, and how to follow the procedures and protocol we were trained to follow. Our individual levels of expertise and what was needed at the moment guided when we led and when we followed.

In node communities, we all have the ability to participate in certain conversations and organizations without an intermediary, but how do we feel, think, and operate when we are on *equal footing* with others? Another essential element of the peer-to-peer architecture is *equipotency*, defined as all nodes within a node community being equally privileged. Each node in a peer-to-peer network is an equal peer node and each node provides their available resources—processing power, network bandwidth, and disk storage—to other nodes. There is no need for any central coordination of resource sharing, and each node both provides and consumes resources.

The Power of Equipotency in Organizations

Organizational equipotency occurs in a coordinated networking system where everyone who works in the organization is working together, *as equals*, toward a common goal. On any given day, I may assume different roles, yet I show up as an equal, regardless of the roles I play. I provide my assets to others, and I accept resources. I can help others. Although my position may enable or impede me from doing certain things at any given time, and work requirements may guide the role I assume, my personhood is always equal to everyone. Neither my role nor my position defines the degree of equality (or lack thereof) that I have as an individual in the organization—each individual serves as an equal and respected peer. I may not contribute the same way others do, but I make my contribution as an equal; I have the same opportunity to contribute, and the manner in which I contribute does not affect my standing in relation to another.

How do we harness the power of equipotency in organizations? In the psychiatric emergency room, we worked together as peers. We shared power and authority—we followed and gave orders as necessary. There was a natural flow to the work and a level of comfort and camaraderie with each other that enabled efficiency, effectiveness, and composure, one crisis and one emergency at a time. In general, equipotency blurs the line between leader and follower, and at the same time clarifies overall purpose within groups and organizations.

All Nodes Are Created Equal: Everyone Leads and Everyone Follows

Cincinnati General Hospital was a training hospital where everyone working in the psychiatric emergency room trained together in various disciplines and specialties. Be they psychiatrist, psychologist, or psychiatric nurse, everyone who worked at the emergency room was there for a common purpose: to be trained in how to treat each patient presented to the psychiatric emergency room. We saw each patient as quickly as possible, made a diagnosis, and provided treatment or referral as needed—all while assuming different roles, sharing information, and listening to our fellow colleagues.

Depending on the day, I could be a member of the emergency room staff team seeing patients as they were triaged, the lead shift person who assigned cases to other staff as they were triaged, or an "on call" staff person, readily available to be called in as needed. The patients' and their families' only concern was that they be given the appropriate treatment by competent professionals in a timely fashion. Having multiple people trained in all the core skills needed in the emergency room allowed for patients to be treated effectively and swiftly.

When we arrived for each shift, there were also no assigned workspaces—no physical division between those with offices and those without, silently and concretely betraying differences in workplace status. Everyone sat in a small room with enough chairs for the staff on duty during that shift, plus just enough counter space for two people. Even the traditional dress differentiation by status common in hospitals did not exist in the psychiatric emergency room. The shared training and shared workspace set the stage for our shared responsibility for completing the task at hand, day in and day out. We showed up as equals and remained that way. In the training situation, and within our small workspace, we were equal by design—all residency trainees working to hone our craft and become a professional in our specialty area.

Driven by Communication (Nodes)

Where positional boundaries inherent in traditional management hierarchies can require certain members to delay action while they await instruction during times of change or crisis, organizational equipotency within a node community allows for team members to respond immediately to the needs of a particular scenario while following and leading as necessary. Normalizing equal footing in working relationships can create an environment where input is genuinely valued and constant communication is encouraged.

Upon arrival for each shift at Cincinnati General Hospital, we would immediately review patient charts, conduct a brief shift transition meeting to make sure everyone was on the same page, and then begin seeing patients. Everyone knew what needed to be done with each patient, and every staff member went about his or her work in a rhythmic fashion. We constantly communicated with each other through conversation, by giving and receiving feedback, and by having dialogue with patients. We also regularly asked for feedback and input from others, from each other, and from other departments in the hospital. Having constant real-time dialogue and feedback improved morale while simultaneously improving team efficiency—everyone knew when they were performing well, and problems were corrected quickly as they were more easily and effectively identified.

The Value of Equipotency in Organizations

Equipotency, as used in peer-to-peer networks, is reflected in the potential strength and valence of involvement by others. Where every person is always equal to everyone else, equipotency (1) serves as an enabler, (2) drives commitment, (3) engenders positive intent, and (4) motivates every team member to give their best. By virtue of showing up in an equal and peer-to-peer way, no one needs to be "empowered" or anointed by someone else. No one has to communicate a vision related to being equal, because everyone already lives, feels, and breathes what that means.

Serving as an Enabler

What is the expected behavior from someone who is told what they can and can't do? And what about someone who can decide on their own or through mutual decision making? Equipotent nodes or individuals have the opportunity to lead and the opportunity to follow—they are expected to solve problems and to learn from their colleagues. Everyone shows up in the same uniform each day—the authentic-self uniform. The outcome is that everyone understands why they showed up, what they need, and what they can do to contribute and be rewarded for success.

Driving Commitment

When everyone leads and follows, the common goal comes into sharper focus. At the Emergency Room, no one had to force or enable us to act on our own. No one implanted a vision within us. Our primary interest in our work, our passion, our commitment to each other, our desire to do well, as well as our desire to help, came from our shared goal and the pleasure taken in knowing that at the end of the shift we had capably managed a series of crises and emergencies for patients and everyone who came through the door that day or evening.

Engendering Positive Intent

Organizational equipotency is intrinsically expressed in mutual respect, confidence, and trust. With no need to compete for standing or individual status, that energy can be leveraged toward the shared goals of the organization. As we rotated from shift to shift and patient to patient at the hospital, we implicitly understood what was expected. We had a keen sense and awareness of the contextual nature of our work, along with the hospital's emergency room's overall mission and goals. Just look at the description of any psychiatric emergency room—where timeliness, quality care, calmness, and collaboration are front and center at every moment.

Motivating Everyone to Give Their Best

What is the real reason for teams looking to work, where each team member is encouraged to act and behave in an equipotent manner? When everyone contributes to the overall success of the organization on equal footing, individuals learn to expect from others what they expect from themselves, and in turn give their best. At the hospital, we celebrated our work and ourselves. Organizational equipotency was reflected in who we were with each other rather than in the assigned work or role. While our daily assigned professional roles were separate from who we were as individuals, the expectations we had of each other were the same as the expectations we had for ourselves. We led and we followed every day, and as such became better at both.

Implications for Organization Design

Today's hierarchical organizations are designed for command-and-control leadership—not equipotency. In addition to the historical roots of command-and-control leadership in organizational life, it is compounded by the long-standing belief and perception that organizations should be structured in a top-down, hierarchical manner either because people want to be led and want someone to tell them what to do, or because they need to be led.

On The P2P Path
BMW Designworks

BMW Designworks is a unique differentiator in the marketplace. Using a concept of cross-fertilization, BMW Group Designworks brings individuals together from a variety of different industries to work on design solutions. They harness global design expertise from around the world and from many disciplines using the design approach based on the precision and detail started with BMW car engineering. The design teams have formed a culture of creative collaboration, and they celebrate creative human talent working from across industries and disciplines on ideas and solutions.

http://www.designworksusa.com

In spite of years of research to the contrary, Theory X is alive and well. Sadly, many workers are now conditioned into this behavior and reject being required to take initiative. They enter the workplace expecting to follow, and on the occasions where they don't, they are often labeled as troublemakers, agitators, poor team members, or heretics.

Inevitably, organizations have been designed to get workers to follow. As Joseph Rost noted, "We still operate in an industrial leadership paradigm. Our current models of leadership shifted primarily our notion of the balance of power and the type of power exerted from command-and-control leadership to more relevance and empowerment, but still dictated by the leader.[11] What changes are needed with current leadership models to understand the important contributions of equipotency in leading toward quality outcomes? Where every dedicated employee walks through the door each day fully vested in their authentic, and non-uniformed self, organizations become more transparent, efficient, and focused on overall mission. We need to challenge ourselves on the rationale for outmoded organizational frameworks that support layers and vertical hierarchies.

Implications for a New Leadership Paradigm

In a peer-to-peer leadership model, all nodes are created equal. All nodes show up and are treated with equal potential and capability in order to contribute to the goals and success of the organization. The accomplishments, work output, and skills are human data points that can be utilized, stored, and organized as well as nurtured, cared for, and nourished.

In traditional leadership models, one individual determines the role of his or her followers. The designation of followers thus given at the door is the designation forever dictating behavior and action. Alternative behaviors can only be demonstrated if sanctioned or allowed by those in power. We pivot one type of leader to another—from one way of working with followers to another—yet one key individual holds the responsibility in determining how followers must act and behave. The "follower costume" is handed to them: their "follower uniform" set by color and design, the space they occupy, and the titles they are given. The "costume" or "uniform" defines follower status and treatment. Ergo, the authentic self must remain outside.

Bottom line? We need to separate the work people do from who they are as humans. We need to recognize that people have the capacity to perform many duties and responsibilities, many work assignments. They should not be put in symbolic straight jackets, required to follow hierarchical mandates, and be dressed in the uniforms accorded them based on duties, roles, and position. While the echo of power and authority and the whispers of how one must act as a leader and a follower lingers in our mind and dominates our behavior, the leader-follower model and the current language of leadership become more and more distant to our everyday reality.

Summary

Equipotency refers to the type of relationship that exists between nodes in any given node community. Nodes within a given community can communicate directly among each other without the need of a central intermediary or any type of hierarchical structure, and the concept of equipotency puts these nodes on equal footing with each other. This equality in standing serves to enable individuals to act as leaders and followers depending on the situation, while engendering positive intent, driving commitment, and encouraging each team member to give their best effort.

The critical question of leadership is how one can demonstrate it when everyone coming through the door does so in an equipotent manner. It becomes a question of how everyone is able to engage in leadership based on their reason for being there rather than their assigned role or position. Leadership shifts based on the particular strengths of individuals and the particular needs of any given scenario. Through processes of real-time feedback between equipotent nodes, the overall mission of the organization is continuously focused and stays at the forefront. Let's now take a look at the ways in which organizations made up of equipotent nodes can and do adapt and respond to an ever-changing environment.

Practical Application

Identify two or three occasions when you have been in an unequal situation or work relationship. What body signals or emotions did you experience? What actions did you take?

Key Points

▶ Organizational equipotency occurs when everyone leads and follows each day.

▶ Practice sharing reciprocity; share your resources with others in order to have capacity to receive from others.

▶ In equipotent node communities, intermediaries are available upon request.

▶ Equipotency is a permanent state reflected in who we are with each other, not what work we do.

▶ The time has come to challenge the rationale for continuing with outmoded organizational frameworks with layers and vertical hierarchies.

4

Relational Dynamics

During the last full week of October 2012, Hurricane Sandy ravaged communities from Jamaica to the northeastern United States—leaving hundreds dead, thousands without food, housing, or power, and billions of dollars in damage done along its path. In New York and New Jersey, flooding and tidal surges devastated coastal and low-lying communities, leaving many residents in need of basic services—something to eat, something dry to wear, someplace warm to go. In the days immediately following the storm, one question almost hung in the air above buildings and neighborhoods seemingly forgotten or neglected by the aid organizations supposedly standing at the ready: Where is the American Red Cross?

It took days before many official responders were up, running, and serving storm victims in the hardest-hit communities, leaving many residents with little option other than to wait. But not everyone was waiting. Anticipating and seeing something of an aid vacuum in the face of urgent and overwhelming need, half a dozen veterans of the Occupy Wall Street movement (yes, the same OWS accused of bringing more heat than light to general debates about the future of the country) headed to public housing projects with flashlights and trays of hot lasagna and handed them out to those in need. Just like that, "Occupy Sandy" was born.

While the American Red Cross was turning away donations and volunteers in the early days of the aftermath of the storm, Occupy Sandy was turning a pair of churches into distribution centers and putting people to work—shuttling supplies to those in need, cooking hot meals, and planning for rebuilding. Volunteers could show up in the morning, go through the same brief training course that every Occupy participant took, and be on the same page as and equal footing with the earliest Occupiers by the

ON THE P2P PATH
GOOGLE

"We don't have business units," Google CFO Patrick Pichette says in an interview with James Manyika. "We're more relaxed. We trust each other. When we sit down to do these allocation reviews, we're all one team with our Google hats on, and the question is what's winning.... People will say, the guys next door are really on fire. They should get the next fifteen engineers. That kind of mind-set gives people the confidence that when they're on fire and things are going great for them, they'll get the capital and engineers they need."

"We naturally attract people who want their financial forecasts to work—and they're going to work like mad to make sure that this only takes one day of their week. Then they're going to spend the other four days of the week reinventing the business, doing crazy analyses that are going to be deeply fact based, in order to find key insights. We naturally attract these people, and because we have them I can close the books in three days. I'm not spending nineteen days closing the books. All of my team is saying 'Alright, we're done. Let's go back to the cool stuff.'"

afternoon. And not everyone was making peanut butter sandwiches, either; from somewhere in the belly of a church, Occupiers organized and coordinated those with needs and those with time and resources to give—a motor pool of borrowed cars and trucks for transport needs, construction teams for mending the broken, and a medical committee for the sick and injured.

It probably isn't a surprise that Occupy Sandy has tech-savvy origins. In addition to serving as general dropoff points for much needed emergency goods, the distribution centers birthed a rapid-response system like no other. With one tweet or Facebook post, Occupy Sandy could alert its whole social network—indeed, its whole node community— to the urgent needs of particular organizations, groups, and individuals. This allowed anyone on the receiving end to offer assistance directly.

If Occupy was short on supplies, it could throw up a digital flag and have donations rolling in quickly. When Occupy Sandy needed specific or higher value items, it used a pretty brilliant strategy: "wedding registries" with a variety of online retailers allowed people who wanted to help but couldn't because of distance or previous commitments to log on and buy something needed and useful.

What seems counterintuitive about the success of Occupy Sandy is that it had never done this before. Occupy Sandy, unlike the American Red Cross and other aid organizations, had no infrastructure, hierarchy, or tangible resources to speak of, but it was still better able to respond to the needs of devastated communities than those long-established entities—and to do it quickly.

Not having leaders meant there was no waiting for higher-ups to give a "go ahead." This allowed Occupiers to make decisions collaboratively and on the fly. Because it was beholden to no real organizational structure, Occupy Sandy was able to function dynamically—to keep the main goals at the forefront and respond to realities on the ground, as they were, instead of acting only in ways consistent with the operation of a rigid organization.

Ultimately, what began as six people, a bunch of flashlights, and a pile of lasagna became one of the fastest, nimblest, and most effective response teams to act during and after Hurricane Sandy—so much so that the American Red Cross actually delivered supplies for Occupy Sandy to distribute!

Relational Dynamics

What does it mean to be dynamic? Does it mean always changing, always ready to change, or always changing directions? Does it refer to the state of things as change is occurring? When I think of the word dynamic, things like movement and adaptation come to mind—specifically dance movements, being nimble, being quick, and adjusting in the moment as things unfold. I think of examples as I work: when I facilitate a meeting or workshop, conduct an Organization Development intervention, or think of a new and innovative way to introduce a new process or method of work. Each requires a certain degree of nimbleness, finesse, and flexibility.

A dynamic action is the action that is needed when you have to improvise in the midst of a facilitation or intervention. To be dynamic is to be prepared and flexible enough to change on a dime because the situation or a combination of factors requires a quick shift away from your original plan. You must be able and prepared to shift—to move seamlessly in another direction—by deftly changing pace. This dynamic occurs at the intersection of art and science.

On The P2P Path
Stiletto Network

The popular book by Pamela Ryckman, *Stiletto Network: Inside the Women's Power Circles That Are Changing the Face of Business*, indicates that women from many disciplines and walks of life are joining together in dinner groups and networking circles to collaborate and to improve and talk about their lives, companies, and communities. A *Forbes* article cites them as "a new kind of networking—power circles that are changing the tone of business." Individuals join the community to connect with others and share advice on anything from careers, handling difficult bosses, and investing to managing child or elder care issues.

http://www.pamelaryckman.com/stiletto-network/overview/

In P2P architecture, the interaction or exchange between peer nodes is a relational dynamic. It reflects an egalitarian network that moves back and forth in a highly effective interdependence and requires complex coordination. Similar to the relational dynamic evident in Occupy Sandy's response to the needs of those affected by Hurricane Sandy, P2P architecture allows for more efficient communication and transfer of information. This happens by virtue of its decentralized and egalitarian nature in contrast to traditional client-server systems models.

The sheer scope of damage done by the hurricane, the urgency with which many who were affected by the storm needed assistance, and the lack of a prompt response by traditional aid organizations required a new relational dynamic among individuals—a dynamic crucial to efficiently and effectively connect those in need to those with time and resources to give. There was no time to wait for large, established, hierarchical organizations to get their acts together, and it turned out that there was little need to do so. No individual person or lone agency had enough knowledge or skill to successfully integrate the critical elements needed to respond to a crisis of this magnitude. The relational dynamic itself was the catalyst for and enabler of the interdependency required, and the relational dynamic allowed different people to act as equals while defining processes, plans, and strategies and working together toward a common goal.

The Value of Relational Dynamics

When hierarchy is absent and nodes are in an equipotent and egalitarian relationship, the relational dynamic itself defines the critical elements and their relationship to each other. There is no leader to pronounce from on high which elements are crucial and which are less so—this makes the question less about who is in charge, and more about what should be done. Organizations themselves are free to react to situational realities as they are rather than as an organization would like them to be. Many channels and routes put forth information, ask questions, and challenge the current state of affairs. All perspectives are heard, integrated, and accounted for—and from this wealth of knowledge and information, main goals and critical elements come into sharper relief. When a node in the same node community as Occupy Sandy gets word that a hospital needs a generator, the relational dynamic is such that it spreads throughout the community and becomes a priority.

People, Information, and Connections

The relational dynamic inherent in P2P networks connects people and makes information readily available to the nodes within a node community. In the case of Hurricane Sandy, the relational dynamic between key connectors was essential because the situation itself required a great level of collaboration, especially since no one individual possessed all the information required to coordinate every facet of the operation. When someone needed to transport pallets of water from one end of New York City to another, it was the relational dynamic itself that allowed the truck-havers of Occupy Sandy to coordinate with the truck-needers. Individual wisdom and the individual leader became an oxymoron and an unattainable feat—and, in fact, with needs being many and varied, the individual leader could have become a self-created bottleneck in an otherwise egalitarian community.

Organizational Anarchy

The knowledge and wisdom generated from the relational dynamic within P2P leadership can become the driver of success. In most organizational hierarchies, the line manager (in positional power) is seen as the leader whose wisdom and input are perceived as superior, because of both position and title within the hierarchy. The input of support staff and others is generally seen as less valuable in relation to the line manager—they are, after all, further down the power chain and perceived as followers rather than as leaders.

This relational dynamic is based on what the higher-ups say is needed when and by whom. It determines what connectors send and receive, and how the connectors must contribute. In P2P architecture, the competence of node connectors themselves is critical to relational dynamics and leads to the right connections being made by the right connectors at the right time, regardless of the connector's position or title. The relational dynamic occurs in the network and the network becomes the leader because actions are based on a consensus of needs.

Here, the word anarchy is not meant in the popular sense of chaos or lawlessness; the anarchy of P2P architecture is anarchy without a designated leader. There is no higher governing authority, but a relational dynamic that emerges between equal, individual nodes, resulting in a higher level of thinking and being—in coming together for the common will or common good. It requires everyone to meet together as equals and be willing to offer and receive ideas and input to reach consensus. Anarchy does not have to be disorder and chaos—if Occupy Sandy is any indication, the absence of a formal leader can be powerful in terms of organizing and collaborating toward common goals.

Shared Decision Making and Governance

In traditional organizations, resources are allocated and approved by certain individuals; if they are removed or denied, workers have no means of contributing or providing resources for others. This is not the case when looking at relational dynamics as an element of complex interaction—there is no one who can decide to cut off or provide resources, as decision making and governance are shared.

In P2P architecture, equipotent nodes control assets; this means that assets available to one node are also available to others. Nodes communicate their needs among themselves, and the relational dynamic between nodes is the connector that enables a common language to be created; it is a complex interaction with other nodes. Rather than looking at relational dynamics as just a social phenomenon, it is viewed as a connector mechanism for assets to be provided and received.

As it stands, organizations have structured relationships for people who work in organizations. These relationships play out in traditional hierarchical roles—there are leaders, and there are followers. In light of P2P architecture, relational dynamics should be considered a key component of organizational design and construction, and they should be based on how equipotent node connectors within the node community form the complex interaction needed to achieve success.

Implications for a New Leadership Paradigm

Leadership is neither a unitary concept that involves one individual demonstrating a set of many skills and competencies nor a set of specific behaviors or personal attributes. Rather, leadership is a concept that can only be demonstrated in the context of a relational dynamic— specifically, when equipotent nodes connect within a node community. Then and only then can leadership emerge. For leadership to be demonstrated, at least two individuals must be in a relationship in which they have an interest, and they need to impact the other(s) in a way that shifts or changes the relationship regarding an outcome. Both individuals must be able to give and receive, and both individuals must expect others to give and receive.

For example, President Obama can only demonstrate leadership when those who expect to be led (or for him to lead) engage with him in this relational dynamic. When Senator Mitch McConnell asserts on the senate floor that the president should lead, that assertion without acknowledging the interrelated nature of leadership is essentially demanding that the president engage in a solo dance or "solitary" act that cannot be leadership. Leadership is only possible with a partner in the dance. The world we live in has changed. If the president engages in a solo dance, he is immediately rebuked for exhibiting poor leadership or a lack of leadership. His politics are then characterized as partisan politics, which roughly translates to "your brand of solitary leadership is not my brand; therefore, I can disregard it as insufficient or nonexistent."

When U.S. House Speaker John Boehner says we must begin to work together, he extends a hand to join the president in a partner dance. He invites another connector to join in the relational dynamic that ignites leadership. Survival of the connected emerges, but can only occur if nodes perceive a need to be part of the outcome perceive the benefits of working together, and seek value in the relational dynamic where leadership as equals emerges.

The beauty of democracy and the U.S. model of governing outlined in the United States Constitution is that it is, by design, structured for the relational dynamic to foster and sustain leadership and common goals. This is a unique element of civil society that allows true growth, liberty, and humanity to be demonstrated. While it can be and is messy at times, organizations must be designed for the same relational dynamic to occur organically within and between organization units. This relational dynamic represents the true evolution from survival of the fittest to survival by connection or survival of a union or bond. Those who truly understand the connected nature of our world are those who move to find the best connection at the right time to move it forward.

Summary

Occupy Sandy's ability to spring into action while traditional aid organizations sputtered to a start shows that the relational dynamic between equipotent nodes can be a powerful force for responding nimbly to crises and matching resources with urgent needs. The absence of a formal leader or chain of command connects people and resources and allows for shared decision making and governance. Nodes are interdependent, and leadership becomes a shared dance of responsibility, resources, and needs. When the structure of the organization itself is no longer the focus, organizations are freed to respond to new landscapes and situations as they are, instead of as their organizational structure would prefer them to be.

Organizations currently operate within a model of survival of the fittest without foresight—without understanding that for an organization to sustain itself as an entity, the natural connections between workers in the organization must be recognized. These connections must occur for an organization to sustain itself and continue to flourish. We no longer live in a world where artificial boundaries can be set up in organizations with the expectation that individuals will dutifully remain within them, or that they are erected for the overall benefit of the organization. Silos must be broken down and interdependence must be seen as a core competency as well as a core value and principle.

Practical Application

Think about a time when you and another person worked closely together to influence a group of individuals so they would do something different. What was the outcome? How could the process have been improved?

Key Points

▶ The knowledge and wisdom generated from the relational dynamic can become the driver of success.

▶ The relational dynamic occurs in the network and the network becomes the leaders so that actions are based on a consensus of need.

▶ A P2P relational dynamic is more than a social phenomenon; it is a connector mechanism so assets can be provided and received.

▶ P2P leadership is a concept that can only be demonstrated in the context of a relational dynamic.

▶ The relational dynamic represents the evolution from survival of the fittest to survival by connection or survival of a union or bond.

5

From Survival of the Fittest to Survival of the Connected

If the story of Dave Carroll and "United Breaks Guitars" showed us anything, it's that P2P networks have made the world vastly more connected than it has ever been. The communicative distance between individuals continues to shrink, and what once seemed a vast and varied global landscape has begun to feel a bit smaller—a bit more like the community market. As many organizations struggle to realize the power inherent in this network, AirBnB harnesses global P2P connections and the accompanying sense of community for the benefit of all "nodes" involved.

As something of an alternative to hotel accommodations, AirBnB allows anyone to list any type of residence for free. Travelers looking for a certain type of place to stay—be it an entire home, a room in an apartment, or a yurt behind someone's log cabin in the woods—can connect with those listing spaces in this P2P marketplace. Potential renters can see pictures and read reviews written by past renters before making a selection, and those renting out places write reviews about the tenants who have stayed there. Taking it a step further, AirBnB allows members to connect a Facebook account so they can see homes being rented or reviews of places written by people in their personal network. It lets them extract travel advice from their personal network. Apart from facilitating payment and offering a space to host listings and reviews, AirBnB largely stays out of the way of a natural P2P process and allows those with extra space to rent to those needing it while fostering a trusted and transparent community through conversation and direct relationships between equipotent nodes.

AirBnB isn't the only company making use of P2P architecture in a meaningful way. To name a few, companies like Relay Rides connect people looking for a vehicle rental with those whose cars sit unused, and startups like Good Eggs work to reduce the distance between grocery shoppers and local farmers, growers, and producers. What does this mean for hotels, rental cars, and grocery stores? These industries are poised for a transformational shift. While the future is always difficult to predict, with the shift from client-server communication to P2P architecture, there does seem to be something of a transition from the survival of the fittest to the survival of the connected.

Darwin Misinterpreted

The prevailing interpretation of the "survival of the fittest" idea—only the strongest survive—is not really based on Darwin's observations from *On the Origin of Species*. Darwin's biological interpretation referred to the ability of a species to adapt to the immediate and local environment when struggling to survive rather than to the preservation of favored races or people who were most physically capable. His biological observations focused on the ability to survive dramatic changes in environmental conditions: how did some species survive things like the meteor impact that resulted in the K-T mass extinction—more commonly known as the event that caused the extinction of the dinosaurs—while others simply went extinct?

Darwin was not referring to who survives; his observation was about how adaptation occurs from an evolutionary point of view. In much the same way that Darwin's observations regarding evolutionary growth are based on how species survive by adapting to changes in their environment, an interpretation of survival of the connected can be today's metaphor to interpret and reframe the notion of how organizations survive and thrive by adapting to changes in technological landscapes.

Adaptation and Mitigation

In a P2P node or network community, there are two critical functions that support the individuals in the node community and the work of the community. These functions are related to connection—one is adaptation, and the other is mitigation. Adaptation is demonstrated when recognition of an impact is based on an event that has already occurred, and a sense of each node or individual being "audible ready" and swiftly moving to action to adapt to current circumstances. A football analogy is helpful; you need to be able to recognize what your opponents are planning to do and able to call a play different from the one you were prepared to execute. In organizations, you need to be prepared for every possible outcome and able to adapt to every situation.

While not as dramatic an adaptation as those required to survive an extinction-causing meteor, the response to the Hurricane Sandy disaster is a twenty-first-century example of adaptation to a mass catastrophe. It illustrates how nodes in a community—not individual people—were able to adapt to the circumstances that existed. In the face of largely unknown and catastrophic circumstances, the Occupy Sandy node community was able to move swiftly by sending and receiving needed information in real time. By facilitating the transfer of information and services between those with urgent needs and those looking to help, the connectedness within the node community allowed for swift adaptation to a quickly changing environment.

Through human interaction and participation, the collective sense of belonging heightened the collective sense of urgency and understanding of the need. Whenever mass destruction occurs, the outpouring of compassion is universally observed. Technology enabled people to act on that compassion by translating the understanding of needs into practical solutions. As a result, the Occupy Sandy node community was able to take action and adapt swiftly. Occupy Sandy was no more compassionate or concerned than the American Red Cross. They were just better able to act on that compassion and concern.

In terms of mitigation, Occupy Sandy learned daily from the changes in their environment and leveraged the observations and vast knowledge contained within their node community. They planned ahead to maximize positive aspects of their daily impact while minimizing negative ones. If trucks or equipment could not get to needed areas because of some barrier or obstruction, real-time communication would allow Occupy Sandy to look for better, more efficient ways to move food, equipment, and materials. P2P connections allowed them not only to take action based on current need, but also to mitigate circumstances and plan for potential unexpected consequences or risks. They were able to enhance resiliency through the promotion of conscious communication and participation; because everyone in the community operated as equal participants in a dynamic relationship, leadership could emerge through the relational dynamic.

Protective Processes

There is research evidence that we are all born resilient—that humans possess an inborn capacity to respond

to circumstances by picking ourselves up (adapting)
and moving forward better than before (mitigating).
The research further indicates that innate resilience is
characterized by social competence and responsiveness,
cultural flexibility (empathy, caring, communication skills),
autonomy (sense of identity, self-awareness, task-mastery,
adaptive distance, and sense of purpose), and goal direction.
Resilience is not something that just a few super-kids
have; it is an inborn capacity that we all possess[12] and is
our own capacity for self-righting, transformation, and
change.[13] Technology enables us to demonstrate resilience
in community with others.

Socially competent individuals have their own identities
and uniforms. They do not wish to wear or rely on the
uniform given to them. When another uniform is forced
upon them, they are likely to resist in many different
ways—some of which (passive resistance, apathy, lack of
motivation) play out in organizational life each day. In
essence, our present-day organizations may be designed
to favor defensive mechanisms rather than the protective
processes that allow individuals to bring their innate
qualities to the workplace each day.

Protective processes are those that foster resiliency and
operate at a deep, structural, and systemic human level—
the level of relationships, beliefs, and opportunities for
participation and power that are parts of every interaction.
Where is it natural to look for strengths and assets, as
opposed to problems and deficits? It's a practice that can be
observed in the way parents interact with young children,
but the corollary is true in organizations that focus on
problems to be solved rather than strengths and assets to be
maximized. The P2P network is equivalent to the protective
process that researchers say enables resilience—caring

relationships with compassion, understanding, respect, and interest—and is grounded in listening, safety, and basic trust.

Solving Problem Solving

Again, the rise of organizations in the mechanizing Industrial Era caused problem solving to be the main lens through which we looked at solving organization problems. Our problem-solving approaches have become very sophisticated and comprehensive, and as long as you have a mechanized-type problem to solve, you can certainly rely on developed and sophisticated tools to solve it. On the other hand, in today's organizations, problems are rarely mechanical. They are almost always complex problems with interrelated causes and many individuals involved in their creation and successful resolution. The sheer complexity and number of individuals involved only serves to heighten their interrelated nature. I became keenly aware of this during the merger of the two large pharmaceutical companies.

When I first joined the pharmaceutical company, there were approximately 40,000 employees. The merger swelled the organization to well beyond 100,000 employees. One thing that I had learned from past experience was that rapid growth in size alone leads to enormous complexity and the need for change. As I began thinking of effective ways to navigate and manage the change that was occurring with the merger, it was clear that existing problem-solving approaches and perspectives would not be effective. The company launched a number of change initiatives that focused on results-oriented approaches, but they were often met with considerable resistance.

As an alternative, we began to look at an approach to

change that did not look at organizations as problems to be solved[14] and instead focused on their strengths. Some team leaders embraced the new approach and began to use it to develop strategies to develop change within their own teams, while some struggled to incorporate it. Other departments perceived the approach as not rigorous enough for solving tough problems, and some senior leadership considered it just another management fad. The approach built on the notion of connectedness within an organization. It enables what Peter Drucker says is critically important—creating an alignment of strengths.[15] Unfortunately, the pharmaceutical company, like most organizations, was not designed for connectedness but rather for structural units with a built-in barrier that prevents the construction of a web of connected strengths. By design, the P2P network community enables an alignment of strengths and allows leadership built on the relational dynamic that occurs through the strength of connectedness to others. This is an important implication for the redesign of organizations and leadership. It is not enough to have new tools and models; we must have a new paradigm for design and leadership. A P2P network community can accelerate the rate of success and achievement of results.

The P2P network community and leadership become linked with each other, as they interact—by giving and receiving. These links weave the cultural fabric of the organization by enabling the creation of more and more links. P2P builds connectedness through human interaction and technological tools for expanding these connections. While the need for resilience is innate, the need for community is universal.[16] We all want a sense of belonging, continuity, and connection with everyone as well as ideas and values that make our lives meaningful and significant.

Summary

Ever-increasing levels of connectivity around the world have shortened the communicative distance between individuals. A new community market exists, and while some traditional organizations still struggle to see the power inherent in the node community, others are already leveraging it—creating node communities around those offering particular services and those with needs for those services. In an ever-evolving technological landscape, it is those who are best connected in the P2P sense who will be best able to adapt to new situations and mitigate the effects of a changing environment.

Though we are all born with the innate capacity for adaptation and mitigation, our organizations are often structured to encourage defensive mechanisms rather than positive connections. Survival of the connected refers to an organization's ability to adapt to and mitigate problems arising from drastic changes in environment. P2P networks enable protective processes that operate at a deep, human, structural level and focus on leveraging strengths of individuals within an organization rather than problems to be solved. Through P2P networks, connections are strengthened through human interaction, and a universal need for community is satisfied. Business objectives and goals can be prioritized, and rapid, informed decision making can accelerate achievement of results.

Practical Application

What protective mechanisms have you observed individuals using when they seem threatened or angry? How might these ripple through a P2P network?

experience, he notes, "People feel like they can bring their whole person to Herman Miller. Combine that with a creative culture that always seems to be trying to reinvent itself in almost anything that it does. People find it's exciting from that standpoint—it always feels like a place that's becoming something."

P2P-structured organizations share precisely that quality of always becoming. Through constant communication and a nonlinear change process, node communities are constantly in various stages of renewal, allowing employees to contribute in a real way to the structure and function of what really is their organization and to play an active role in shaping its culture and priorities. The sense of shared ownership coupled with constant improvement makes for a positive experience for many.

Summary

The P2P Network Community is more than a social network, it is also a workflow network. Much of the power of the node community is in its ability to be dynamic and to shift according to a set of principles that guide how information is sent, received, and organized. Where traditional organizations have inherent communication boundaries in many of their structures, P2P organizations are nimble in their ability to respond to changing environments. Where traditional organizations tend to practice linear processes of change, change within the P2P network community is constant, making the devotion of time and space to plot organizational change unnecessary. Change becomes a natural state within the network community.

The P2P network community can be aligned with many of the existing change models. In terms of the evolutionary model, P2P networks are constantly changing based on the input of member nodes and changes in environment. P2P networks are nothing if not dialectical, as nodes are in constant, direct communication, enabling and encouraging regular discussion and debate surrounding ideology and mission. The teleological model becomes interesting as the network becomes the leader and community moves toward goals and results. In the P2P network community, the renewal of organizational culture, values, and rituals in line with life cycle and cultural models take center stage.

Practical Application

Write a metaphor or a story that depicts your mental model for change. What are some ways your organization could become more nimble?

Key Points

▶ Nimbleness is a unique feature of change within a P2P network community.

▶ Behaviors and actions that must be planned as major change in traditional hierarchical organizations are part of the natural state of a P2P network community.

▶ The concepts of time and space are redefined in a P2P network community.

▶ In a P2P network community, building a productive workplace and sustainable organization is the process.

8

Real-Time Feedback and Dialogue

Sally appeared at the door of my office and wiped tears from her eyes with a tissue. "Come in and have a seat," I said. She sat down and tears began to flow more heavily. I handed her a box of tissues and remained silent. After a couple of minutes, she looked up and said, "Thanks for letting me come in without an appointment. I just finished my performance review with Sarah Jane, and I'm so upset." She began to recount her experience of the meeting. "Sarah Jane told me that others had reported to her that my performance was poor and my attitude was not good. I'm blown away! I had no idea what she was talking about. Last year, Jim was my supervisor, and my performance review was excellent. None of my ratings were below a 3 (out of 5 scale), and the comments about my behavior were very good as well. Sarah Jane came in a few months ago and immediately began assigning work to John and Marsha. The three of them had worked together before in another area. I didn't have any meetings with Sarah Jane until we had a customer issue, and she asked me to do the investigation and prepare a report. There were a number of corrective actions that needed to be taken, so I included them in the report and sent the report to Sarah Jane and the heads of the two departments that were also involved. I've had no other interaction with Sarah Jane until today." Unfortunately, Sally's situation is not atypical and might even have occurred in your organization today.

Providing feedback to employees is a widely discussed and somewhat controversial topic. Most employees say they want open, honest feedback, and most organizations have elaborate processes for providing feedback to their employees and training on how to give it. Still, many studies have shown that performance feedback rarely improves performance, and there always seem to be calls for the end to performance feedback as it now exists in organizations.

So what is the problem? Why is it that after years of HR departments developing feedback tools and systems to encourage feedback and managers taking the time and committing to providing feedback to their employees, we still have a feedback disaster on our hands? The answer to that question is at the heart of why we need another structure for working together—a structure that is built around the spontaneous, real-time delivery and reception of feedback and input.

The more traditional attitudes and beliefs about employee feedback can be heard and felt in comments such as: "Why should I give someone feedback or pat them on the back for doing the work they are supposed to do?" Sentiments like, "We're here to get work done, not hand out praise" are not unusual in many conversations. "I don't want to single one out and be critical." The result is often no conversation, or a tone or manner of offering feedback that belittles and undermines. Most feedback comes from the boss, so the situation in which it is given is very charged. Criticism, sarcasm, and personal judgment can often lead to anger, frustration, and disappointment on the part of the person receiving it.

The problem is not that feedback should be given or not given; rather, the formal or informal system of giving feedback is so mechanical, convoluted, and likely to be perceived as disingenuous that no one is comfortable giving it, and few appreciate the intent in doing so. Often, more attention is given to shortcomings than to contributions and accomplishments. Most forms of organizational feedback turn out to be criticism and personal judgment that all too often carry an emotional underpinning. In our current age of constant feedback and input, this belief and behavior is completely foreign to many new workers. They give instant feedback and expect instant feedback. The challenge now to optimize feedback so it will be most efficient and effective. I'm optimistic that as we transition into network communities, the human instinctual nature of being in community and dialogue will advance civil feedback.

New brain science is giving us a glimpse into why our current system of feedback is not effective and should be retooled.[24] Neuroscientists have identified that our brains have certain protective defense mechanisms that are unconsciously activated when we perceive a threat to our sense of self. If taken the wrong way by those on the receiving end, what might begin as well-intentioned feedback can actually put up physical and biological walls that are difficult to take down.

Starbucks: Two Observations, Two Outcomes

My neighborhood Starbucks was the place I did most of the writing for this book. For ten months, two or three days per week, I spent three to four hours at Starbucks with pen and pad, sipping a Grande Soy Chai or Very Berry Hibiscus (or several of them, depending upon how long I stayed). During that time, I had the opportunity to observe just about every employee working different shifts and performing different duties; I found myself as eager to observe what was going on around me as I was to pull out my Moleskine® journal and start writing. After a few months, two primary observations and what seemed like a potential opportunity for a field research study stood out. I became aware of two distinct types of behavior, depending upon which associates were working certain shifts.

The first observation I made was that there seemed to be a definite shift in mindset, employee attitude, and commitment to tasks that occurred once Howard Schulz returned and launched what he called his "back to basics turnaround."[25] The seven thousand-plus stores in the United States were closed for a three-hour retraining session for baristas. The retraining was a strategic move by returning CEO Howard Schulz to accomplish what he called "regaining the soul of the past," which included returning to the original Starbucks culture of entrepreneurship, creativity, and innovation. That might not have been the case in other Starbucks cafés, but it certainly was in the one in my neighborhood. I have lived in the neighborhood for a long time and witnessed the transition firsthand.

On most days, employees seemed content to carry out their specific responsibilities. Baristas called out the name of the person whose order was ready, in addition to clearly and consistently calling out the name of the product they had ordered. The baristas paid close attention to each order and the details about steamed milk and espresso. The cashier always clarified the order to make sure it would be prepared properly, and employees smiled when they arrived at work, during their shift, and as they departed. They usually said goodbye to everyone before they left. They would all chat with the regulars, and the short exchange never interrupted the speed of service. In fact, you could tell by their expressions that the regulars enjoyed being recognized. When the cashier would ask someone something like "Regular Mocha Latte today?" the person would smile as though their day had been made richer by those few words.

On The P2P Path
NYU – A Global Network University

In 2010, President John Sexton announced that New York University, the largest independent research university in the United States, was embarking on a new project—becoming a global network university. This new project will create a structure that allows students and faculty to gather in various locations around the globe. The idea flows naturally from the eco-systemic relations that NYU has always had with New York City as a university in and of the city. With the introduction of NYU as a global network university it will become a university in and of the world. Diversity of thought, international connections, and faculty collaborations will abound across and between locales around the world.

Students and faculty will be able to join communities and work with peers across various disciplines, locales and formats—virtual or onsite within NYU sites or with partner institutions to learn, exchange research ideas, develop integrated curriculum, or convene individuals to discuss critical societal changes.

http://www.nyu.edu/students/graduates/
global-network-university.html

During one visit, one of the associates—after having seen me writing so often—asked if I was writing something. I said yes, I was working on a book about peers and leadership. The associate smiled and began telling me how important leadership was at Starbucks. He told me how the values of Starbucks were taken seriously and that the very words were printed on their smocks. One wonders how many employees in other organizations know exactly what the company vision is and how they can demonstrate it each day—even without pointing at the words on their uniform, but just by the way they treat each other and their customers.

Over time, it was easy to see that Starbucks provides customers much more than a good cup of coffee. When the order line was long, someone came from behind the counter and began taking orders from customers as they waited. When there was no line, I regularly saw someone grab a broom and clean supplies with which to tidy and restock the condiment and service area. Trash was emptied and tables cleaned. The employees all smiled and seemed to enjoy their work, and on most occasions, it was difficult to tell who the supervisor was. Associates seemed to exchange duties and requests with each other.

The second observation I had was that direct feedback was given only during some shifts and came from one supervisor whenever he was on duty. While most of the time I couldn't tell who the on-duty supervisor was because of the pattern of interaction, I could tell one individual was a supervisor from his behavior and the way he gave feedback to other associates. When he was on duty, he would stand behind the workers and tell them what they should be doing or ask why something was not being done.

Most associates seemed able to respond to his direction as well as to focus on the customers, but on a few occasions it was clear from the non-verbal expression that what he was directing the associate to do was not what the associate thought should be done (even though they always followed his direction). When this individual was there, business was still efficient, and customers still received their orders in a timely fashion, but the associates did not talk as much with each other or with the regulars when he was around. When he was there, he was often in the back office and rarely seemed to check the traffic or help when it was very busy.

Occasionally, I wondered if there was a difference in sales or quality of work during the shifts that the associates worked seamlessly and did whatever was needed to take care of customers as compared with shifts where the supervisor in charge was providing feedback and direction. Given what we know about feedback, it would not surprise me if there was a difference—if not in actual sales, then almost certainly in the customers' perceptions of workers during shifts that the supervisor was giving feedback. The real-time feedback among associates that occurred when he was off-duty was almost certainly more effective for the overall operation of the Starbucks than anything he ever seemed to contribute by way of direction.

A Better Way

For feedback to be helpful, it must be perceived as respectful, timely, specific, and needed. Like Sarah Jane and the Starbucks supervisor, each of their behaviors was consistent with what one would expect from an organization with a traditional structure where the supervisor had responsibility to provide feedback. They were the supervisors in charge, discharging duties and responsibilities as they perceived them to be or as they had been taught. The HR practices and processes in place may even reward this behavior to a greater extent than that of supervisors who encourage employees to work as peers with their co-workers.

At the same time, the Starbucks experience during most shifts—shifts where the one supervisor was absent—closely resembled the workings of a P2P network community. There were many who behaved in a responsible manner. The Starbucks associates ensured everyone was responding to customers and their needs. They monitored the quality of the product. They attended to efficiency, and they ensured a clean environment. They sent and received information to and from one another as equals; they worked closely in a relational dynamic with one another based on business needs in the moment, and this allowed the network community to demonstrate leadership as needed without any real need for a formal leader. As in Occupy Sandy, the network itself was the leader.

Real-time feedback and dialogue among associates occurred throughout the shift and undoubtedly helped each associate to complete their duties and contribute to knowledge about customers, products, and each other. While it is easy to make these observations in a small retail establishment and think about it as a network community, imagining real-time feedback and dialogue in large organizations may be more challenging. However, following the basics outlined in a P2P network community, real-time feedback does not have to be the daunting task that it is in traditional organizations.

In a P2P network community, there is no delay in feedback because all members of the community are sending and receiving information all the time. Real-time feedback and dialogue occur every day, all day long. When something is shared or passed along to someone else, they can accept it immediately, respond to it, add to it, or use it. Members of the network know clearly what they are working toward and what is necessary to accomplish their goals. They seek information, share it, and retrieve it on an as-needed basis. Everyone in the network works as an equal member of the community, so there is no need to wait for direction.

For example, Carol worked at a large, multinational consumer products company. She retrieved some information from a colleague, James, that he had posted on the company intranet. The information helped her understand a problem she was having with a client. As soon as Carol received the information, she immediately let James know she had picked it up and how useful it had been for the work she was doing with her client. James could see that she had retrieved the information, and he was glad it was helpful to her. She also told James in her email that she especially liked the way he had linked several pieces of data together and that she would like to pass some of the information along to another colleague, Jennifer, who was working in a different group on a new format for profiling a new customer base. She thought this information could be helpful to him as well. James replied that he was delighted. He told Carol that he would be more than happy to assist Jennifer because he had previously worked with the target population while doing another job.

Interestingly, Carol is located in Lucerne, Switzerland, which is James's manager's home base. At coffee a few days later, Carol saw James's manager and mentioned how helpful the information had been to her.

Now, you might say that this could happen in any organization, and while you would be correct, the fact is that with today's organizational structures, this occurrence is quite rare—and if it is not rare in a particular organization, it is likely more dependent upon the manager and the relationship he or she has with a particular employee than it is on retrieving and sharing information.

When organizations are designed so that employees know there is a time and place for feedback, they will generally look for that time and place. When feedback occurs outside of that specific day, time, or arena, it may never get passed along or shared with anyone since there is no expectation, and in many instances no incentive or desire to do so. That is why it is so important to design organizations that facilitate and encourage this type of behavior by using the natural flow of information and making it easy to pass along.

Carol's quick move to share information with Jennifer and Carol's response to the information she received from James was an example of adaptation. Receiving information from another node (individual) in the community gave her the ability to build capacity. Passing it along to Jennifer was an example of the power of mitigation. Carol prevented Jennifer from reinventing something that had already been done, helped her learn how to do something she had not done before, and sped up the time it might take Jennifer to complete her assignment. This increased the overall efficiency of the organization and strengthened collaborative bonds between coworkers. All this feedback and dialogue conveyed valuable information about workflow. It was more than just a social exchange among peers—it was a transfer of information and skills between equals working toward a common goal.

Additionally, Carol and Jennifer were able to access the information they needed as a result of technological advances. Data mining and data analysis provide real-time data in all areas of business, and there are many applications on the market now that capture data that can be analyzed quickly and disseminated for use around the world. One example is Jabberly,[26] an application that allows people to use their mobile devices to ask questions about what is going on at particular venues and other entertainment locations and get answers in real time. What makes this application different from some of the information available on places like Yelp and Foursquare is that they incentivize people to provide information as well as retrieve information. Rewards that can be used as a sort of social currency increase the amount and quality of available information. Jabberly is an excellent example of a technology that will enable the shift to the new paradigm of a P2P network community—a network community that will be able to gather and use information in real time. The challenge is to design organizations that can enable real-time feedback and dialogue.

Summary

As real-time feedback applications become more mainstream and their use in businesses rises, there will be a greater call for feedback processes within an organization to be revamped completely. Workshops on constructive feedback, giving and receiving feedback, and managing difficult employees through feedback will be tools and techniques of a bygone era. They will be replaced with real, live people in a network community who give continuous feedback to peers in real time.

The days when one had to plan to give someone feedback and wait until a formal performance feedback cycle came around will soon be gone. For feedback to be useful, it needs to be perceived as respectful, specific, timely, and needed. Within P2P architecture, members of the network will be able to provide and solicit feedback when they need it, and the vast majority of feedback will be informative and positive. As in most human interchanges, there will be little need to be critical or disrespectful or to rely on personal judgment to communicate with someone. Feedback will be less about what is going wrong, and more about what is going right and how particular processes or information can be improved.

In the last few chapters, we have looked closely at specific value propositions of particular elements of P2P architecture. From real-time feedback to nimbleness to change and from efficient flow of information to the survival of the connected, each element of P2P architecture holds certain benefits for communities. In the next two chapters, let's look at implications of P2P architecture on leadership and organizational structure.

Practical Application

Tell your best and worst feedback stories. How might the ending of each have been different in the context of a P2P relationship or organization?

Key Points

▶ Performance feedback and performance management tools are controversial and too often do not provide an increase in performance to match the investment a company makes in them.

▶ Some research has found that performance feedback decreases performance.

▶ Many employees perceive performance feedback as criticism and personal judgment. This can be met with distrust, anger, and frustration.

▶ Neuroscience gives us a glimpse at why current performance feedback systems are ineffective.

▶ Real-time feedback is naturally-occurring, organic feedback that is more often positive than negative.

▶ Data mining and data analysis tools are now available for real-time feedback and dialogue to occur within organizations.

▶ The challenge is to design organizations that enable the interface of individuals and technology.

9

Implications for Organization Design

I once worked in a large hospital system in the southeastern part of the United States when it was forced to respond to the threat of managed healthcare—a phenomenon that swept healthcare in the United States during the 1990s. The hospital system's response was to merge with a rival hospital in another part of the city. The merger, billed as "a merger of equals," was an extremely difficult undertaking, and the two institutions eventually de-merged. One remarkable lesson I learned from the experience can be found in the "story of the turkeys."

In the midst of the largest of cost-cutting initiatives, a decision was made to eliminate the traditional distribution of holiday turkeys to every employee. Because the merger would double the size of the newly formed health system, the cost of the turkeys would double, and because the other hospital had no comparable practice, it was deemed an unnecessary expense that could be eliminated. A few dissenting voices from the senior leadership team protested; however, finances were the most important criterion used to determine what stayed and what was eliminated.

The day the announcement that there would be no turkey distribution for Thanksgiving was made, it was as if a war had erupted. Protests came from all parts of the organization. Passionate employees made very eloquent pleas about the bigger meaning of the turkey distribution and what the organization was losing. They spoke about how some employees had donated their turkeys to their favorite charities every year so that those less fortunate could look forward to a meal; they talked about how the turkeys were a reflection of the culture and all the people who worked there. The outcry was so impassioned and sincere that the decision was almost immediately reversed.

After hearing how people felt, it was hard not to appreciate the value of symbolism and small demonstrations of caring. It was clear that there was something bigger driving the behavior of those who bothered to speak out in protest. It was coming from a place beyond what had been envisioned in the executive room when the decision was made. In taking only the cold numbers of the merger into consideration, the executives had no idea what they were actually eliminating when they decided to strike that item from the budget.

That day taught me that people can engage in their work as passionately as they engage with their loved ones and those they care most about. It was another opportunity for me to pause and ask: What were we doing that kept that behavior (that appeared almost instinctual) below the surface? How could we design an organization that would allow that passion to be demonstrated all the time?

Successful P2P organizations will create environments that allow this kind of culture to flourish. Their mission will be aligned with the values of their employees, because employees will be equal participants in shaping the form and trajectory of organizations. The misunderstanding about the meaning of one turkey a year will almost never happen, because there won't be a backroom meeting of executives with priorities unlike those of the rest of the organization.

Why Is P2P Architecture Important?

We are almost certain to continue to experience more environmental, economic, political, and social unrest as the world changes and continues to grow. In a world

of constant and often rapid change, organizations must
be adaptive, resilient, and innovative. Large and small
organizations alike are influenced by global reach in the
expansion of their businesses, in dealing with internal
and external customers, and in dealing with suppliers in a
global marketplace. Heightened competition from around
the globe requires most organizations to be more efficient,
especially as it relates to customer response and access to
products and services. The data deluge from many sources
has not matched our ability to discern, interpret, and use
data in the most efficient and effective manner. The human
element of engagement in organization life needs to match
the technological penetration and capacity that now exists.
As individuals interact more and more with technology,
we need to ensure there is greater alignment and synergy
between the two. Both must enable each other. Individuals
must use technology more efficiently and effectively and
technology must enable human capacity to flourish.

We need less central authority and power, and fewer
levers of control. The search or quest for a new approach
intensifies and looms over us. From a P2P perspective, the
design question becomes: How do we design organizations
as networks that connect in a way that facilitates our
abilities to adapt and self-correct? How do we design
organizations that are as resilient as possible?

For years, our organizations have operated like
orchestras, in which the conductor, like the CEO, is seen
as the most important person on the stage. The role of the
conductor is to interpret music. Little is left to chance.
Flawless execution and timing are the most crucial
qualities of orchestra players. In an orchestra, everything
is predictable. Members who display creativity are not

welcome, and pieces are played as the conductor interprets the original work.

A P2P network community, on the other hand, is more like an improvisational jazz group, in which a small collection of musicians starts with rhythm and melody and then plays spontaneously. In the jazz group, creativity emerges and moves along through improvised melodies. It is not about being better; it is about improving by trying— by going outside the lines, by bending the rules to make a different or improved sound. In the orchestra, boundaries are set. Jazz musicians create sounds that intertwine and play off of each other. This way, musicians often discover sounds that might not have been heard before. New music— new processes and new solutions—can be heard each time someone plays. Strict adherence to the form is not as critical as in an orchestra, and therefore one's ability to generate something new and innovative can thrive.

In the jazz group, as in the P2P network, the journey is more fluid, even as the relational dynamic is exciting, fun, and energizing. Even with this freedom, the starting rhythm and melody give the piece an origin and some sense of direction. In terms of organizational design, the elements that bring form and color to an otherwise shapeless and varied network of equipotent nodes are the work experience and the work environment.

The Work Experience

In our department at New York University (NYU), my assistant and I routinely spend our days at different locations. If she has work to do at our 12th Street building, she simply logs in online when she arrives. If she has to be at one of our main campus buildings for an evening event with potential students, she again logs in from wherever she is and logs out when she leaves. My responsibility, as Department Chair, is to ensure that the work is getting done as expected and designed, not to monitor her comings and goings. She has the freedom to alter the way she works, when she does her work, and how she accomplishes tasks. She seeks my assistance as needed and provides me with

ON THE P2P PATH
Hot Spots Movement

Launched in 2006 and based on a book by Lynda Gratton of the London Business School, Hot Spots Movement is a blog devoted to highlighting collaborative work practices and providing guidance on how "hot spots" of innovation, excitement and productivity can be cultivated within your organization. She introduces the reader to her research and gives examples on how it can be applied for deeper understanding of the value created by cooperating with, listening to, and dialoguing with others. A recent post says:

So, what do organizations do about these paradoxes and how can they truly understand what drives their Gen Ys? PwC's Next Gen report has a few recommendations, but one stands out to me as particularly important for this fast-moving, tech-savvy group: "Invest time, resources and energy to listen and stay connected with your people."

http://www.hotspotsmovement.com

input as she thinks necessary or when I request input from her. She has a designated workspace but often uses the community workspace at another location. This is her typical work environment today. As an employee who is subject to the wage and hour laws in the United States, she is required to monitor her work hours closely; however, NYU has systems that allow her to both meet the wage and hour requirements and maintain the level of flexibility she needs to accomplish her tasks, even in different locations.

In a typical neighborhood, small village, or city, people all have their own points of origin or "home bases," but they are not always there. They visit other people and other neighborhoods; they go in and out of neighborhoods and villages for specific purposes. You might go to a local neighborhood restaurant to eat and join friends, to a different neighborhood to see a movie or concert, or to a specific area for shopping or antiquing. You might attend a university or community college for your education, professional development, or trade skill; you might meet with people from other neighborhoods to collaborate on city-level projects; you might check on your elderly neighbors to make sure they are okay.

Communities within P2P network organizations will be similar in function to neighborhoods, villages, or cities. The neighborhoods will be for, and work toward, specific purposes, and will allow individuals to move from one community to another based on need and purpose. You might start in one location but move back and forth freely based on what you have to do that day. You would not clock in each morning to restrict movement. You would clock in to indicate the start of your workday, and you might clock in from any location on a mobile device. If you work on equipment, your start time may be indicated when you first sign on to the console or start the equipment. Meetings within P2P organizations will be impromptu, be scheduled as needed to accomplish goals, and use a variety of communication tools to ensure that everyone who needs to be present can be present. The forced weekly meeting with the boss will be another remnant of the past.

In P2P organizations, individuals move freely throughout their work environment. They have a home-based network community with a work program based on objectives, goals, and strategies defined by the network communities to which they belong. Technology is used to monitor and document. Individuals, as nodes in their community and other communities, understand the work requirements and hold themselves accountable for the work result, using private places or public spaces based on their work.

The Work Environment

In a P2P network organization, communities have many locations available to them, some of which are private, while others are public. The locations designated as private are places within the organization where individuals—as parts of the node community—can have private meetings or engage in personal activity (e.g. lactation, personal communication, reflection, or quiet time). These are designated as "private places" and are available to any member of the community as needed. Locations designed to be public are areas where work and leisure occur in collaboration with others. Public spaces may be anything from open cubicle areas, hotel units, libraries, and patios to flower gardens, coffee or tea bars, art galleries, racquetball courts, or table sports areas. The P2P work environment is designed for connection, collaboration, and conversation.

The work environment is designed to enable the workflow that requires dynamic movement of people and information. Some equipment may be stationary, but people and information must be able to move freely.

In Google's New York office, public spaces are bright and airy, with plenty of room to sit, work, and play. It is just as common to see employees playing pool as sitting at desks in a cubicle. At Google's Mountain View complex, employees have door-to-door services as well as workout and personal care facilities on the premises. Meals are subsidized, and cafeterias boast enticing food options from around the world. The work environment is designed for workers' convenience and to ensure continuity between work and personal life. As such, it fosters connections within the organization.

In much the way that rigid meeting schedules and personal monitoring of clock-in times become less important in a P2P organization, offices with fixed boundaries, rigid space allocations, and minimal public space will also be relics of the past. Employees will have a choice of workspaces and move from service areas and the manufacturing floor to an abundance of public spaces. They will sit in open cubicle areas similar to the original designs of Herman Miller, in offices as needed, and in comfortable chairs in public spaces. Similar to the shared common areas in a house or on a university campus, the majority of work space will be public, meaning employees will be free to work wherever they want.

Coffee breaks as we know them now will also likely cease to exist because coffee and tea bars, small cafes, and places that serve breakfast, snacks, lunch, and dinner to go will be a part of all large organizations. The large, industrial-appearing factory floor areas where employees must take their breaks will be replaced with smaller, more homelike, more informal sitting areas. The freestanding vending machines and metal chairs of office buildings past will be replaced with self-serve areas similar to those now found in some hotel chains, where guests can step into the kitchen area and help themselves to snacks, fruit, and drinks. The new atmosphere is meant to give the feeling of walking into your own kitchen, library, or quiet corner. Fortunately, many organizations are being designed to be more open and employee-friendly work environments.

P2P organizations will know what is important to employees. They will not have incidents like "the Turkey Story." They will understand that for centuries, meals have been times for people to come together and break bread as equals. Gathering places will be designed as such. Cafeterias will have conference kiosks for small meetings during a meal and tables where families can join employees for lunch. The executive dining room, C-Suite, and corner office will give way to common dining areas, many suites, and common offices to enjoy the views and reflect on your work alone, or with others.

Though work experience and environment will both be integral to the survival and function of P2P organizations and network communities within the organization, the sheer diversity within each organization will almost guarantee that no two organizations will share the same expression of these elements. The work experience and environment will be concrete reflections of the passions, mission, and culture of each organization.

While maintaining the individuality of organizations, P2P principles will ensure for some common elements shared, and there will be many implications for organization design within a P2P network community and P2P organization. Organization charts and histograms will be rendered obsolete. Organization design will need to be a multidisciplinary discipline in which organization development and work design specialists, interior designers, architects, and landscape artists all work together. Flexible work arrangements will become the new normal, and total compensation will be comprised of many factors—some fixed, and some that may change based on workers' lifestyle changes or business needs of the network community. Individuals will need to be recruited to join a network community based on doing a specified cluster of tasks rather than being hired for a specific position. Individual work schedules may vary throughout the year or time spent in a community; they may be full-time, part-time, flexible shift, sabbaticals, or virtual.

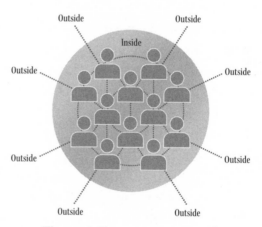

Figure 4: Peer to peer network

Summary

The P2P organization will have a set of organizing principles that align with the organization's vision, mission, and goals, and guide governance and policy development around two core elements: the work environment and the work experience. Successful P2P organizations will be those that create an environment where a genuine culture develops based on strong connections and human interaction.

The work environment is the element of organizational architecture that defines the spatial aspects of the workplace. The work experience will be designed around equipotent network communities aligned with the strategy, business imperatives, and human needs of the members of the community. Whether it's McDonalds or McDonnell-Douglas, Boeing or Boloco, Murray's or Michaels, Blazestage or Blazerunner, Delta Airlines or Delta Faucet, BMW or WMB—all organizations can be designed to meet the needs of those who depend on their services or products and those who choose to enter their virtual doors each day to work.

Unlike the industrial era of design that many organizations still reflect today—the era of private spaces (square offices with or without windows) separate from public places (lobby and cafeteria)—the new P2P organization will be designed with approachable private places and many public spaces. Each community will be connected by a robust technology infrastructure that enables maximum connectedness and communication, and an open framework that invites participation by all.

Practical Application

Take a sheet of paper and draw a line down the middle.
Label the left side Work Experience and the right side Work
Environment. List all the things in your organization that
you find appealing about both work experience and work
environment. Read the list, share it with a colleague, and
have a conversation about how you could improve both
without spending any money. Ask others to do the same
exercise. Share your ideas.

Key Points

▶ The P2P organization is designed for organizational
form and function. The two primary functions
are adaptation and mitigation. Adaptation in
the P2P organization translates to the means to
productivity and achievement of results; mitigation
translates to the means to innovation.

▶ The P2P organization is built to align the
organization's vision, mission, and values with two
core elements: the work experience and the work
environment.

▶ The work experience defines how members of the
network will work together in a relational dynamic
environment where everyone works as an equal
participant.

▶ The work environment defines the spatial, physical,
and aesthetic elements of the environment.

⑩
Implications for Leadership

Tom Watson Sr., the founder of IBM, once said in an interview many years ago that he wanted IBM to be like an "industrial family"—a family where your duty is to those you serve and to those who work in the organization.[29] For years he focused on IBM customers and on fair compensation for employees, and that became one of the things IBM was known for as it grew to become one of the most successful and influential companies in the world. Tom Watson Sr. also introduced the THINK concept—an idea where he made sure every employee was encouraged to bring ideas forward every day. THINK signs were posted everywhere so employees would see them no matter what direction they turned. THINK became known as a symbol of IBM.

Tom Watson Jr. expanded on his father's legacy and added a focus on social issues that affect organizations. In addition to all employees being encouraged to bring their ideas forward, he introduced other changes that related directly to respect for the individual. He eliminated the hourly wage that distinguished one class of employee from another; he introduced tuition loans for employees; and he introduced the annual company survey where employees gave feedback on the managers, the company, and the workplace as a whole. All employees rated their manager, all other managers, the division, the region, all the way to the chairman's office. They rated the facilities and the workplace and could also write in comments. The annual survey was taken very seriously, and employees could see actions being made at all levels of the organization as a result of their feedback. To the chagrin of many employees, the original employee survey and the practice of listening to the voices of all employees were discontinued. As the company grew and changed over the years, the survey morphed into a representative sample of employees providing limited feedback. One can only wonder and speculate on the unintended consequences and actual cost to the organization of diluting employees' voices, especially for those who lived in THINK culture. IBM and a few other U.S. companies were unique in their leadership approach, and they were revolutionary in their time.

Traditional business leadership grew out of the Industrial Era, when challenges required a response that maximized standardization, operationalization, and hierarchy. Our traditional leadership theories and approaches were designed to address the priority needs of the Industrial Era organization. They have served the organization well, but these priorities are largely at odds with the world today. Today we have less and less central authority and power, fewer levers of control, and diminishing resources. There are many new and complex problems to solve—from global population growth, urbanization, and the need to create employment opportunities to the interconnectedness of the world economies, political transitions, and the growing influence of China and India. All are challenges that did not exist in the Industrial Era, and these new challenges require a new response and a new form of leadership.

The time is now, and the quest for a new approach intensifies and looms over us. We must acknowledge the shift and translate insights and new ways of working into policies and governance. Leadership must be both understood in a new way and expressed in new ways. It must be more transparent, collaborative, and flexible. We must acknowledge that our industrial era of leadership and design is an outmoded remnant of past grandeur. It is not serving us now and will not do so in the future. The companies that have endured are aware of what foundational elements made them great and which of those threads can be interpreted in light of today's challenges.

Organizations are systems not unlike other natural systems that have a development cycle and path. Individuals start organizations for a purpose, usually from an idea for a product or service. They get others who are interested in their idea to join them. The core of the organization is built from its original purpose, its raison d'être, and that reason is integral to every organization's foundation.

Our prosperity provided a new lens to look at public organizations. Milton Friedman, a Nobel Prize–winning American economist, wrote that the sole purpose of the organization was to provide a return to the shareholders. Until recently, this was the primary lens through which many viewed their role in the organization—to preserve shareholder value at all costs. Events of the last few years have caused the pendulum to shift away from Friedman's view and look more to the earlier views of Adam Smith; his views on capitalism and modern economic theory are more reflective of the purpose of the organization talked about by many founders of U.S. companies. The P2P network community and P2P organization are built upon the premise that economies and organizations are strongest when their purpose is to serve a common good rather than self-interest.

Organization Formation

Development of the P2P network community is different from the development of individuals within the organization. The organization network community is a whole system that develops itself as an entity—an entity comprised of many network communities that are all connected and working toward a common good. The P2P organization network community is more than the sum of the individual nodes or individuals within the organization. It is an entity comprised of many network communities that operate as systems within a larger system and are all working toward a common good for all those who are being served by and all those who serve the organization.

For a P2P organization network community to achieve excellence and overall success that will be sustainable over time, it must reach a level of maturity where all network communities work toward a common purpose or mission. In a P2P network organization, this level of maturity is reached through a developmental path defined as organization formation.

Organization formation is comprised of four stages required to reach a level of maturity and leadership necessary to achieve excellence and overall success that will be sustainable over time:

Stage 1 – Internalization of values and purpose,

Stage 2 – Mutual and continuous exchange of input and output,

Stage 3 – Reconciliation of polarities and abstractions, and

Stage 4 – Formation of dyad exchange structures

Organizations must successfully go through stages one through three before they can achieve ongoing and sustainable success at stage four—which is the process whereby two individuals influence a group of individuals to achieve a common goal. The formation of dyad exchange structures is demonstrated by the catalytic action that occurs in the relational dynamic between two nodes (individuals). The natural order of the organization is to work toward a common goal.

External and internal forces will influence when and how organizations go through each of these stages. Critical success factors in reaching stage four are awareness and an understanding of the necessity of ensuring that each of the first three stages are woven into the fabric of the organization. These three stages must be present before they can reach stage four, where dyad exchange is necessary to achieve success—as evidenced by Occupy Sandy and many responses to natural disasters. Many companies have come close over time, but only a few have succeeded in a sustained way.

One example of stage one—mutual and continuous internalization of values—is Johnson & Johnson, the large multinational pharmaceutical, consumer goods, and medical devices organization founded in the United States in 1866. Johnson & Johnson recognized the importance of internalizing of values and purpose for long-term sustainable success. The J&J credo is carved into the wall at the company's New Brunswick, New Jersey headquarters. It stands as a symbol and guide that challenges all J&J employees to put the needs and well-being of the people they serve first. Robert Wood Johnson, former Chairman, wrote the credo in 1943, just before the company became a publicly traded company. It was and still is considered a moral compass for the company. Many believe it is the secret ingredient of their success.

J&J employees are proud of the credo and the guidance it provides. Every two years, employees complete a survey to voice their opinions about how the company is doing with regard to the credo's values. Ethicon Endo-Surgery, a J&J company, was my first major employer after graduation. During the entire time I worked at Ethicon Endo-Surgery, I kept a copy of the credo in my calendar. It remained there until I no longer carried an ink-and-paper calendar. I am sure my experience is like that of many current or former J&J employees.

The power of the credo was also noted by Collins and Porras in their classic book, *Built to Last*.[28] One of the poignant insights in their analysis was that truly great companies do not define profits as the driving value of their business. Rather, by the indicators they used, companies that perform best over time aim to bring value to their employees, customers, and community. Johnson & Johnson has never wavered from their original credo and purpose. The credo is reinforced year after year. It is part of the DNA of the company.

Another example is SAS, the American analytic software and services company. When Jim Goodnight, founder and CEO, learned that one of his key executives was pregnant and had announced that she wanted to leave to be home with her newborn child, he decided to build a childcare center on the SAS campus instead of accepting her resignation.[29] This response was consistent with his overall philosophy and vision for the company and with the purpose for which the company was built: "that you really have to give people a great place to work." Throughout his tenure as CEO, he has done just that.

Stage two—mutual and continuous exchange of input and output—is reflected in Google's leaders, Sergey Brin and Eric Schmidt. Their insistence on the possibility of "skip level" conversation, willingness to respond to communication from employees, and policy of encouraging workers to take initiative, be creative, and learn from each other embodies a leadership model that fosters mutual and continuous exchange. Permeable boundaries and fluid conversation is a footprint of their style and culture.

SAS can be cited again as an example of Stage three—reconciliation of polarities and abstractions. Jim Goodnight takes his role as steward of the company vision and purpose very seriously, and this commitment is reflected in his decision to not become a publicly traded company. As the company grew, there were undoubtedly pressures to do so. Jim Goodnight recognized the polarity between his purpose and the vision of a publicly traded company. He reconciled that polarity and achieved the success he sought for his company. Each year, SAS is recognized with awards from around the world. In 2013 alone, Fortune named the company as number two in its list of the best companies to work for in the United States. SAS was among China's

ON THE P2P PATH
ROWE

Results Only Work Environment is an innovative work environment where everyone is in control of their own work schedule. The focus is on results. For those who have jobs that do not require face time, ROWE is a counterculture work practice. Launched at Best Buy and later abolished, ROWE has been launched in other companies, including the Gap headquarters. Employees are paid for output—not for showing up. Companies are reporting improvement in employee engagement and satisfaction. Productivity improvements are less clear but seem to be emerging in companies that are using data analytics to measure outcomes.

http://www.gorowe.com/main/what-is-rowe/

top employers for the sixth consecutive year. Germany named it the number three IT Company. It was also named a top employer in Brazil, and Norway ranked the company second best among its workplaces. It has grown consistently since its founding; the employee turnover rate is well below the industry average for other software firms. For many years, it has been on the Fortune list of the one hundred best companies to work for. Goodnight is by no means a traditional leader, and in many ways SAS seems as though it is definitely on the path toward becoming a P2P organization.

Human Resources and Organization Development

For quite some time, HR departments have supported the achievement of purpose and mission in the organization by developing policies, processes, practices, and programs that are primarily focused on helping the individual improve in order to achieve desired goals and results. There are recruiting policies and procedures, performance management policies and procedures, employee orientation procedures, compensation and benefits strategies and procedures, and policies to ensure compliance with laws and regulation. There are work councils, unions, and ombudsmen.

In recent years, HR has become more involved in providing direct support at the business unit and organization level by strengthening its focus on employee engagement, talent and succession planning, and development of leadership programs. In general, these initiatives are part of the HR strategic direction aimed at supporting the organization's broad goals and strategies.

The HR strategy is implemented through a series of HR initiatives or programs that are sponsored and implemented within HR. In practice, they are usually more operational and tactical than strategic. The degree of influence and the level at which HR fully supports the overall organization strategy is evidenced by the reporting relationship and participation at the executive level of the organization. This varies widely across organizations.

Organization Development, as a discipline, supports the achievement of the organizations' purpose within the context of planned change, systems intervention, and social justice. Unlike HR, which is primarily focused on the individual, organization development is concerned with the whole system. System interventions are focused on preparing the organization for change in readiness or effectiveness. They also focus on strategic alignment with organizations' missions. What is often missing in the theories and approaches of both HR and OD is a clear articulation of the level of organizational maturity needed to engage in operationally focused programs and initiatives designed to help them achieve their desired results.

Organizations that have not reached stage three of organizational maturity will have considerable difficulty building organization effectiveness initiatives, regardless of how well-planned they are. The results will either be short-lived or result in complete failure and significant costs to the organization—costs that may take years to recover. Some organizations cannot recover, and some have gone through the stages of organizational formation better than others. For many, the results may have come more from unconscious competence than from a conscious awareness of the development path they followed. This concept is reflected in those organizations that continue to be successful even when there is a change of top leadership, like GE and Herman-Miller. For others, success has come from skilled organization development practitioners and change experts who have studied how organizations evolve and how they can change. The experts in the field have built much of the foundation necessary for the P2P organization, the P2P network community, and P2P leadership. Their insight has guided and influenced my practice and work.

Questioning Traditional Leadership

The National Leadership Index[30] is an annual study that analyzes United States citizens' confidence in leadership across thirteen different sectors. It shows that sixty-three percent of Americans do not trust what business leaders say, and eighty-three percent believe that leaders work to benefit themselves or a small group, not society overall. The most recent findings note a decline in the belief that America is suffering from a leadership crisis, down from seventy-seven percent to sixty-nine percent. Though this percentage is still considerably high, it may be an early sign that the influence of Milton Friedman, the financial crisis, and the transparency of corporate wrongdoing is shifting the tide of the purpose of a "public company." Eighty-one percent of Americans believe the nation's problems can be solved with effective leadership, and sixty-one to eighty-eight percent believe ordinary citizens have a great deal of power and responsibility to help solve these problems. This is a sign of optimism and an excellent call to action for effective leaders.

There is no agreement among researchers or practitioners about the definition of leadership, and there is even less about which approaches produce the greatest success. Northouse[31] defines leadership as a process by which individuals influence a group to achieve a common goal. He further outlines leadership as a complex process with many dimensions that are of crucial importance to the success of any organization. There are historically distinct approaches that focus on traits, behavior, situational, contingencies, or cultural values. Some are more popular than others, and some have influenced practice more than others. Most are either individual-centered (and thus value-based) or relationship-based.

In spite of the proliferation of newer approaches and the focus on principles, virtues, and individuals, there is still considerable concern about the existing state of affairs. Each of these leadership approaches provides excellent guidance and direction to inform designated leaders about the characteristics that reflect the core values of most organizations. There are also compelling approaches that put stewardship, relationship, and interaction in the foreground of leadership. These new approaches clearly recognize the importance of collaboration and open sharing. However, the "leadership practice in use" continues to be focused on individual leaders and on command-and-control leadership. Even though most of the popular approaches have replaced the authoritarian behavior characteristics of command-and-control leadership with more benevolent, compassionate, and ethical forms, these approaches are still expressed individually by too many of those in formal positions of authority.

Each approach continues to describe the relationship between the leader and the follower in terms of what a "leader" should or should not do as it relates to followers. A discussion of followership has never reached the level of importance given to discussions of leadership, again reinforcing the notion that leadership is a top-down or bottom-up relationship—not an equal relationship. Many of these leader-follower approaches also continue to, by default, reinforce some of the traditional artifacts of the earlier approaches that focused on the "great man." Research studies have found that women leaders are often excluded from strategic informal networks or "old boys' clubs." In these instances, the hierarchical model of leader and follower may perpetuate the glass ceiling, despite the noble attempts that have been made to break it via organizational change. Network communities are beginning to address the issue in different ways.

The time has come to completely rethink our notions of leadership and recalibrate them with the realities of today. Individual-centered leadership is becoming a myth found in textbooks more than a reality—virtually nothing can be done completely independently anymore. Fortunately, leadership has the potential to both frame relationships that will allow organizations to achieve excellence and establish what those relationships will look like within the twenty-first-century organization.

P2P leadership outlines a new view with significant implications for leadership in the future. It presents an opportunity to shift the current landscape and focuses the concept of leadership in a fundamentally new direction. The P2P network community is the product of the evolution of organization structures that are facilitated by technologies that transcend time and space. A P2P organization network community is built by the design of the community as well as by the information exchange and by relationships that form through equipotency and relational dynamics; it is aimed at achieving a common good for all. In such a community, leadership emerges in a new way.

Leadership as a Dyad Exchange Structure

P2P leadership presents a new way to look at and think about building and achieving organizational excellence and success. P2P leadership surfaces within the relational dynamic of an organization's network community and evolves as the organizational entity develops and equipotent nodes interact as equals working toward a common goal. P2P leadership is demonstrated by the catalytic action that occurs in the relational dynamic between two individuals (dyad exchange structure) working together toward a common goal. It is not an elitist perspective where power and importance is implied, nor an approach that espouses togetherness or partnership but fails to address the inherent problem with the hierarchical nature of the leader-follow model. It is not restricted to one individual, and there is no separate distinction between those that are leaders and those that are followers.

The foundation of P2P leadership is derived from an understanding of organization formation and the developmental characteristics required for effective leadership. By using technology and the connectedness of a network, dyad exchange structures are capable of demonstrating leadership all the time, in many different ways, and under many different circumstances. Everyone sends and receives, and everyone leads and follows. This structure enables the dance of leadership through organization design. As was the case with Occupy Sandy, those involved in the dance are so connected that they can adapt to and mitigate circumstances as they occur.

We can return again to the example in the Cincinnati General Hospital Psychiatric Emergency Room where individuals who worked together were able to demonstrate leadership. Work as colleagues enabled each of us to build the dyad exchange relationships necessary to achieve excellence. We were prepared to operate on near-autopilot as individuals or nodes that gave and received as equals.

Another strength of the relational dynamic is that it is capable of correcting itself or self-righting when overturned or disrupted. Because of the strength of the connections between nodes, and as a result of constant real-time feedback, problems are identified and addressed as quickly as they arise. Where traditional leadership often requires the creation of space and time to plan for changes in an organization, P2P organizations are in a constant state of renewal, and P2P leaders will understand that their job is not to centralize, but to facilitate and encourage the effective and efficient use of resources among equipotent nodes in a particular community.

Summary

The new paradigm for leadership is a dyad exchange structure—the process that occurs in a P2P network community when two individuals help a group or community of individuals achieve a common goal. This new form of leadership allows us to move beyond the Industrial Era concept of leadership. P2P leadership is not about someone leading and others following. It is not about eliminating the role of CEO. It is about changing the nature of the relationship between all those who work in an organization. The individual-centered, command-and-control models of leadership are outmoded and must be replaced. The organizations that survive will be those that study the foundations that made them great and reinterpret those foundational elements in light of today's challenges.

Organization formation is made up of four stages necessary for an organization to reach full maturity and be sustainable over time— internalization of values and purpose, mutual and continuous input and output exchange, reconciling polarities and abstractions, and forming dyad exchange structures that connect nodes for the purpose of resolving polarities and innovating.

Trust in traditional business leadership has hit near-historic lows, but the majority of people still believe that leadership plays a role in solving many of our problems. That being the case, the vast majority of leadership theories still focus on leadership of individuals and reinforce traditional relationships between leaders and followers. P2P leadership is a new model of leadership—one that creates space for the types of connections needed to leverage an organization's inherent strengths.

P2P leadership is a dyad exchange structure that relies on the catalytic action that occurs in the relational dynamic between two individuals; it strengthens the bond of connectedness and enables the network to do its work. It embraces advances in technology as extensions of our capacity to evolve as humans in a connected world and rejects the notion that leadership should be limited to the individual or defined in terms of command and control.

Practical Application

Identify the level of maturity your organization has reached. What are the implications for the future success of the organization?

Key Points

▶ Our traditional leadership theories and approaches were designed to address the needs of the Industrial Era organization, and these priorities are largely at odds with the world today.

▶ P2P leadership is a new paradigm defined as the catalytic action that occurs in the dyad exchange structure—the relational dynamic between two individuals working together toward a common goal.

▶ P2P leadership follows a developmental path to organizational maturity.

▶ Organization formation is the developmental path that leads to maturity, a common purpose, and a common good for all those who serve and are served by the organization.

▶ The evolution of organization structures facilitated by technologies that transcend time and space produces the P2P network community. The network is the leader that supports P2P leadership within the network community.

Moving Forward

One of the most exciting and fulfilling assignments I ever had was to design and staff a corporate daycare center. Chelsea Square was an experiment in innovative design and innovative early childhood education. It served children of professional parents from three months to five years of age. The children were diverse, and their parents were equally diverse in age, professional occupation, ethnicity, and religious affiliation. The center was located in the downtown business hub of a large Midwestern city. It was open, airy, visually engaging, and, for maximum security, completely transparent. All entrances, furniture, fixtures, and accessories were child sized and child friendly. The bathrooms were unisex and had no doors. Parents were welcome and invited to visit often. There was a library so parents could read to their children when they came to visit and space for parents to eat lunch with the children. A quiet room for lactation was near the nursery. The atmosphere was relaxing and inviting. Toys, tools, and materials were everywhere, and the large multipurpose playroom had bright painted murals and hidden obstacles. Friendly faces and helping hands were omnipresent. The nursery cribs had matching sheets, rocking chairs, music, and mobiles.

One of the more unique features of the daycare center was the Pre-K classroom. At miniature desk tables, IBM PS/1 computers sat neatly on the desks alongside the markers, crayons, thick pencils, and cases that held a selection of

educational game floppy disks. Each morning the four-
and five-year-olds planned their day with their teacher
and decided what computer work they would do that day.
On any given day, it would appear that this activity was as
natural as frequent trips to the potty unaccompanied by an
adult. But this was not always the case.

The decision to install computers was a topic of much
discussion among the teachers and early education
specialists charged with designing the curriculum and
school programs. The education specialists were convinced
that computers were here to stay and were a means for
young children to learn important pre-school concepts and
skills. Computers were designed to be fun and easy to use.
They were simple to set up, required little attention, and
were tools to build confidence and prepare children for their
first school experience. Computers were the future.

Teachers, on the other hand, were less enthusiastic and
quite reluctant to embrace the new tool. "We're doing just
fine with the materials we have. These children have enough
gadgets and gimmicks at home. They don't need them here."
It was clear: the teachers were perfectly content with their
methods and loudly voiced their disinterest. They spoke
about the lack of research to support the hoopla and media
hype about something that had never been used in the
classroom.

Before Chelsea Square opened for children, you could
hear teachers whispering to each other as they organized
and personalized their classrooms. "I just don't think it's a
good idea to bring a machine into the classroom. They will
break within a few weeks and detract from the skills we
need to teach. Anyway, when will we be trained? I didn't
sign up to learn how to use a computer. I'm a preschool

teacher, not a computer teacher." Another unspoken fact
was that none of the teachers had ever used a computer,
and most were concerned about not being able to master
the skills needed to teach the children. They did not voice
their concerns openly, but their behavior and expressions
reflected insecurity, incompetence, and ambivalence about
their level of control in the classroom.

The decision was made to equip the Pre-K room with four
new IBM PS/1 computers and a selection of educational
games on floppy disks. The greatly-anticipated computers
arrived. Two teachers did not show up for work, and the
remaining teachers from every classroom looked on with
a variety of facial expressions: wary, petulant, confused,
excited, fearful, confused, and tepid, to name a few. When
the last computer was installed, the IBM representative
announced they were ready to use. One of the teachers
spoke up. "We haven't been trained." "No training necessary,"
replied the IBM sales representative. All expressions shifted
in unison to shock and amazement. "When the children
arrive, just turn the power on and put one of the floppy
disks in the drive. Watch me." He looked at the teachers
and assured them the children would be fine—they would
figure out what to do and help each other. He suggested the
teachers just observe the children to see what choices they
would make. Each day, the children discovered something
new. A month later, a parent stopped in to talk to a teacher
and commented, "Ryan says he taught Sally and Miss Patti
how to make the animals talk." The expression on her face
was priceless.

I didn't know it at the time, but I was experimenting
with my first P2P network community. If we fast forward
to today, it is clear that technology must guide how

organizations prepare for the future. CEOs expect technology to drive the most change in their organizations over the next three to five years,[34] and they seek a greater level of understanding of what changes are needed and how technology can most effectively facilitate them. P2P leadership is built on the premise that our new, connected era is fundamentally changing how people engage, and organizations must respond accordingly. P2P leadership provides a new level of understanding. Organizational openness offers tremendous upside potential, but it also builds anxiety in organizations concerned about perceived vulnerability from openness. To recognize and mitigate risks associated with increased openness, technology can provide the analysis needed to quickly uncover patterns and identify potential risks. Analyses and business data will provide a platform for a new organizational architecture and infrastructure.

Organizations must not merely feel comfortable doing business all around the world, with many different cultures, in many different settings and locations, but must also embrace the expanded global community. Growth in China, India, Turkey, the United States, Brazil, and the United Kingdom will fuel the need to be more innovative when building and expanding existing companies and operations. Struggling small- and medium-sized organizations and large enterprises will need to find ways to improve performance and maintain their market position in an ever-changing social and technological landscape. Entrepreneurs who launch new companies will need to have a clear path to success and a clear understanding of how others will help them pave that path.

Before P2P, inequality was ensured by design. From rigid work hours and segregated cafeterias to separate elevators, entrances, floors, and restrooms, separation and inequality abound in many twenty-first-century organizations. Internal divisions no longer serve to strengthen an organization.

ON THE P2P PATH
Paul Polman at Unilever

Ending quarterly earnings reporting and treating small tea farmers the same as shareholders: this is Paul Polman's signature. He is the CEO of Unilever, the company best known for brands: Dove, Becer, Hellman's, and Lipton Tea. Since 2009, when Polman moved into his new role, the goal has been to return the company to its roots and purpose and restore long-term sustainable value. He notes that social cohesion is one of the biggest challenges facing organizations and that consumers want to know how people are being treated along the entire value chain.

Tea farmers work directly for Unilever rather than for an intermediary tea business. Unilever trains the tea farmers in soil management so the tea farmers get a greater yield, and Unilever has a sustainable supply of tea. Everyone benefits. The company reports revenue quarterly and earnings at mid-year. Unilever's share price has doubled since Polman joined.

http://www.theglobeandmail.com/report-on-business/careers/careers-leadership/paul-polman-rebuilding-capitalism-from-the-basics/article9577971/

Instead, they can make it more difficult for a traditional organization to respond to rapidly changing environments. P2P network communities allow equal institutional membership. The network is the future for organizations, and the network itself will be the leader. Organizations will strive to reach the maturity phase of organizational formation (level four)—P2P leadership demonstrated as a dyad structure that enables the organization to achieve the success it desires.

Through a strong network of direct connections between individuals as equipotent nodes, the network will facilitate the efficient transfer of resources and knowledge to meet pressing needs. In this way, leadership will emerge from different areas of the organization as it becomes more nimble and more able to fully leverage its strengths. The critical question for the future becomes what can be done in organizations to move in the direction of the P2P network community and be on the P2P path. It's not a question of whether organizations will have to adapt to a P2P landscape, it is just a question of when.

For those of you who are doers, there are many concrete steps you can take to begin the P2P discussion in your organization. Conduct regular town hall or assembly gatherings to bring everyone together to hear key messages and to reinforce and acknowledge the reason you are all together. Listen to everyone and their ideas, and use analytic and technological tools now available to make sure all voices are heard and shared. Show up each day as a role model, and hold yourself accountable for P2P leadership behavior.

You can talk about the purpose of the organization and why it was started, ask others if they understand the original purpose and agree with it, thank everyone whose actions support that purpose, and work to remove any clearly identifiable barriers to equal participation while inviting others to join you in doing so.

You can talk and listen to individuals at all levels of the organization. Introduce regular breakfast or lunch meetings to talk with employees. Arrange for your own education and training on P2P organization networks and write down how it will benefit you and the organization. Walk around the building and look at everything you've never seen before. Every day, introduce yourself to someone you don't know. Sit in the cafeteria. Ask for advice from someone outside your main circle. Celebrate a failure and discuss what you learned from it with a colleague. The P2P network is strengthened only by direct, human contact between equipotent nodes. Acting that way can set an example for colleagues and begin to break down internal barriers to communication.

If you are a thinker, find areas within your organization that look like P2P networks and watch what happens. Find ways to join in or incorporate those behaviors into your work. Think about a result or goal that your organization is trying to achieve and make a list of all the information you have that might help. Look for parts of your organization that reflect the outdated approach to leadership. Think of a few things that you would like to see changed and have a conversation with someone who has similar thoughts. Visit a competitor or two and see if you can observe P2P characteristics; talk with someone about how they could fit into your organization.

Ask yourself what would need to happen to make your organization a P2P network community. Visit the parts of your organization where you observe P2P network activity and think about the impact they have on the organization. Think about what information you have that you could make better use of. Try to reframe problems. Think about the assumptions you make and how they would change under P2P leadership. Think about things in the organization that are hidden or under the table and how they would surface in a P2P network community. Reflect on your thoughts and share with them with a trusted colleague or friend.

If you are a helper, remember that it is natural to need help from others and to want help. Practice seeking help before trying to help others. Ask someone for opinions and advice on an idea you have or a project you are working on. Follow their counsel and observe what happens. Keep a journal of everyone who asks you for help. Read the journal at the end of each week. When you seek help, practice being clear about what help you need and how the other person can provide that help. Be mindful of your expectation, and pay attention to the entire process of seeking help, explaining yourself, and receiving help. Watch to see who seeks you out and what type of help they seek from you. Join others who reach out for help and join others who help.

Peer-to-peer organization network communities are already among us, and paying closer attention to them will help us understand how we can best transform some of our existing organizations as well as start new ones. P2P architecture is slowly but surely becoming the way in which our world is organized and connected, and it seems that not even banking institutions will be immune. Bitcoin, a UK-based, open-source, P2P digital currency company has allows individuals and organizations to make instant, P2P transactions with no central authority and all transactions carried out by the network. Banks in a truly P2P economy would have to be entirely reinvented if they were to exist at all. In a world moving toward the survival of the connected, many well-funded, largely hierarchical organizations that are "fit" by most measures of business fitness may find themselves in serious need of change if they are to survive, let alone thrive, in a P2P landscape.

It is really not a matter of whether or not P2P architecture is going to have some larger impact on organizational design; it is much more a matter of when. From Occupy Sandy to AirBnB to the social media storm caused by Mitt Romney's threat to fire Big Bird, there are numerous examples of the power that P2P architecture already holds in our lives, and the examples only multiply. Instead of trying to fit the new natural order into the rigid workings of a traditional organization, P2P leadership recognizes the power inherent in the network and works to leverage its collective skills for the benefit of all.

Like the teachers who were reluctant to introduce computers into the Chelsea Square classroom, we have a choice about how to look at P2P architecture. We can decide to not show up for work, resist the new technology kicking and screaming, and have it leave us by the wayside as our mode of doing business goes extinct, or we can decide to relinquish command and control. We can choose to let the technology be the conduit through which organizations are strengthened. Through building a network of individuals of equal status who are directly connected to one another, the P2P network is really becoming the leader.

Notes

Chapter 1

1. Kurt Lewin and Dorwin Cartwright, *Resolving Social Conflicts and Field Theory in Social Science*. Washington, DC: American Psychological Association, 1997.
2. Ira Chaleff, *The Courageous Follower: Standing Up to and for Our Leaders*. San Francisco: Berrett-Koehler, 2009.
3. Barbara Kellerman, *The End of Leadership*. New York: HarperBusiness, 2012.

Chapter 2

4. Louise Gikow, *Sesame Street: A Celebration of 40 Years of Life on the Street*, New York: Black Dog and Leventhal Publishers, 2009.
5. Rüdiger Schollmeier, "A Definition of Peer-to-Peer Networking for the Classification of Peer-to-Peer Architectures and Applications." *Peer-to-Peer Computing*, 2001. Proceedings. First International Conference on IEEE, 2001. 101-2.
6. "Romney's Threat to Big Bird Sows Confusion Abroad, and Feeds It at Home," *New York Times*, accessed June 6, 2013, http://thelede.blogs.nytimes.com/2012/10/05/romneys-attack-on-big-bird-sows-confusion-abroad-and-feeds-it-at-home/; "Could PBS Profit from Mitt Romney's Debate Comment About Big Bird?" *TIME*," accessed June 6, 2013, http://business.time.com/2012/10/04/savit happened: Second pup-boosting-pbs-fundraising/; "As it happened: Second presidential debate" *Financial Times*, http://blogs.ft.com/the-world/2012/10/second-presidential-debate-live-blog-part-two/
7. "I am Facebook friends with Ryan Lanza," *Salon*, accessed June 6, 2013, http://www.salon.com/2012/12/17/i_am_facebook_friends_with_ryan_lanza/; mother jones lanza site
8. Frans Johansson, *The Medici Effect: Breakthrough Insights at the Intersection of Ideas, Concepts, and Cultures*. Cambridge: Harvard Business Press, 2004.
9. Malcolm Gladwell, *The Tipping Point: How Little Things Can Make a Big Difference*. Boston: Little, Brown, 2006.
10. Malcolm Gladwell, "Six Degrees of Lois Weisberg." *The New Yorker* 11 (1999): 52-63.

Chapter 3

11. Joseph C. Rost, *Leadership for the Twenty-First Century*. New York: Praeger, 1991.

Chapter 4

Chapter 5

12. Emmy E. Werner and Ruth S. Smith, *Overcoming the Odds: High Risk Children from Birth to Adulthood.* Cornell: Cornell University Press, 1992.

13. Werner and Smith, *Overcoming the Odds.*

14. David Cooperrider and Diana D. Whitney, *Appreciative Inquiry: A Positive Revolution in Change.* San Francisco: Berrett-Koehler Publishers, 2005.

15. Peter F. Drucker, *The Effective Executive: The Definitive Guide to Getting the Right Things Done.* New York: Collins, 2006.

16. R. J. Lifton, "The Protean Self: Human Resilience in an Age of Transformation." 1993.

Chapter 6

17. "News & Broadcast - World Bank Broadens Public Access to Information," accessed June 6, 2013, http://web.worldbank.org/WBSITE/EXTERNAL/NEWS/0,,contentMDK:22635372~pagePK:64257043~piPK:437376~theSitePK:4607,00.html.

18. "Google's CFO on growth, capital structure, and leadership," *McKinsey & Company*, accessed June 6, 2013, http://www.mckinsey.com/insights/corporate_finance/googles_cfo_on_growth_capital_structure_and_leadership.

19. "Here's A Google Perk Any Company Can Imitate: Employee-to-Employee Learning," *Fast Company*, accessed June 6, 2013, http://blog.fastcompany.com/post/46341828275/heres-a-google-perk-any-company-can-imitate.

Chapter 7

20. "Interview with Dr. Kurt Bock in the Swiss newspaper *Finanz und Wirtschaft*," BASF: *The Chemical Company*, accessed June 6, 2013, http://www.basf.com/group/management-interviews/bock_fuw_1212.

21. Edgar H. Schein et al., *DEC is Dead, Long Live DEC: The Lasting Legacy of Digital Equipment Corporation.* San Francisco: Berrett-Koehler, 2004.

22. Schein et al., *DEC is Dead.*

23. "How Herman Miller Has Designed Employee Loyalty," *Fast Company*, accessed June 6, 2013, http://www.fastcompany.com/1689839/how-herman-miller-has-designed-employee-loyalty.

xx. Ronald J. Burke, Mitchell G. Rothstein, and Julia M. Bristor, "Interpersonal Networks of Managerial and Professional Women and Men: Descriptive Characteristics," *Women in Management Review* 10.1 (1995): 21-7.

Chapter 8

24. Roberta Conlan, *States of Mind: New Discoveries about how our Brains make Us Who we are.* New York: John Wiley, 2002.

25. "Howard Schultz on How to Lead a Turnaround," *Inc.*, accessed June 6, 2013, http://www.inc.com/magazine/20110401/howard-schultz-on-how-to-lead-a-turnaround.html.

26. "Jabberly," *CrunchBase* profile, accessed June 6, 2013, http://www.crunchbase.com/company/jabberly.

Chapter 9

Chapter 10

26. "IBM100 - A Business and Its Beliefs," accessed June 6, 2013, http://www-03.ibm.com/ibm/history/ibm100/us/en/icons/bizbeliefs/.

27. "Thomas J. Watson Sr. Is Dead; I.B.M. Board Chairman Was 82," *New York Times*, accessed June 6, 2013, http://www.nytimes.com/learning/general/onthisday/bday/0217.html.

29. "How SAS Continues to Grow," *Inc.*, accessed June 6, 2013, http://www.inc.com/magazine/201109/inc-500-james-goodnight-sas.html.

28. Jim Collins and Jerry I. Porras, *Built to Last: Successful Habits of Visionary Companies*. New York: HarperBusiness, 2004.

30. S. A. Rosenthal et al, "National Leadership Index 2009: A National Study of Confidence in Leadership." (Cambridge: Center for Public Leadership, Harvard Kennedy School, Harvard University. 2009), 3.

31. Peter Northouse, *Leadership Theory & Practice*. Thousand Oaks, CA: Sage Publications, 2013.

Moving Forward

32. George Pohle, and Marc Chapman, "IBM's Global CEO Report 2006: Business Model Innovation Matters." *Strategy & Leadership* 34.5 (2006): 34-40.

Acknowledgments

No words are sufficient to acknowledge my gratitude and debt to the many colleagues who encouraged me to write and helped whenever I asked. For all their direct contributions and gifts of time and caring, I am deeply humbled by and appreciative of Marc Gerstein, Art Kleiner, Ed Schein, Dick and Emily Axelrod, who helped me get started; Peter Roche, Ruth Danon, Doug Couturier, and Patti Wuennemann, who provided wonderful advice, support, and material; and Gemma George, Pauline Fernandes, and Cathy Royal, friends who were always there to listen to and encourage me.

My debt to mentors, colleagues, and friends in OD, especially W. Warner Burke, Barbara Bunker, Billie Alban, Karen Davis, Denny Gallagher, Peter Block, Fred Miller, Judith Katz, Charlie and Edie Seashore, Marv Weisbord, Sandra Janoff, Brenda B. Jones, Ron Ashkenas, Peter Sorenson and Theresa Yaeger, David Jamieson, Bob Marshak, and Geoff Bellman, who have been wonderful teachers throughout my career. This book could not have been written without their wisdom.

My gratitude to Tom Thomson, who has been a cherished friend, colleague, source of intellectual support, and thought partner for many years and has always provided excellent insights just when I needed them.

To Neal Maillet, Jeevan Sivasubramaniam, and the entire Berrett-Koehler team: your welcome to the BK community and your advice, counsel, and encouragement have been more than I could ever have imagined. Thank you. All of you have made writing this book a pleasure that I will always cherish.

To Clarence, Chuck, Darryl, Asuka, Celessa, and Piper, whose hands and heart touch me and this book in so many ways everyday: thank you for everything.

Index

Note: an *f* after a page number indicates a figure.

About the Author

Mila Baker is Associate
Professor, Academic
Chair, and Director of the
MS in Human Resource
and Organization
Development program
and Interim Director of
the MS in Management
and Systems program at
New York University's
School of Continuing and
Professional Studies. She
has over twenty years of
experience in leadership
roles in large multinational
organizations, including Ethicon Endo-Surgery (a Johnson
& Johnson company), Pfizer Inc., the Dana Holding
Corporation, and Senior Consultant/Advisor at the World
Bank in Washington, DC. She lives in New York City.
Baker holds an MA and PhD in Clinical Psychology and
Organizational Behavior from the University of Cincinnati
in Cincinnati, Ohio, and is a licensed psychologist.
She is a Past Chair of the Organization Development
Network and a past Board member of Human Resource
People & Strategy. She is also a member of the Academy
of Management, the National Training Laboratories

Institute, International Leadership Association, American Psychological Association and the Society for Human Resource Management.

Reach her via

Twitter: milabakernyc

Email: Mnb5@nyu.edu

Linkedin: www.linkedin.com/profile/ view?id=7723349&trk=nav_responsive_tab_profile

Berrett–Koehler
Publishers

Berrett-Koehler is an independent publisher dedicated to an ambitious mission: *Creating a World That Works for All*.

We believe that to truly create a better world, action is needed at all levels—individual, organizational, and societal. At the individual level, our publications help people align their lives with their values and with their aspirations for a better world. At the organizational level, our publications promote progressive leadership and management practices, socially responsible approaches to business, and humane and effective organizations. At the societal level, our publications advance social and economic justice, shared prosperity, sustainability, and new solutions to national and global issues.

A major theme of our publications is "Opening Up New Space." Berrett-Koehler titles challenge conventional thinking, introduce new ideas, and foster positive change. Their common quest is changing the underlying beliefs, mindsets, institutions, and structures that keep generating the same cycles of problems, no matter who our leaders are or what improvement programs we adopt.

We strive to practice what we preach—to operate our publishing company in line with the ideas in our books. At the core of our approach is stewardship, which we define as a deep sense of responsibility to administer the company for the benefit of all of our "stakeholder" groups: authors, customers, employees, investors, service providers, and the communities and environment around us.

We are grateful to the thousands of readers, authors, and other friends of the company who consider themselves to be part of the "BK Community." We hope that you, too, will join us in our mission.

A BK Business Book

This book is part of our BK Business series. BK Business titles pioneer new and progressive leadership and management practices in all types of public, private, and nonprofit organizations. They promote socially responsible approaches to business, innovative organizational change methods, and more humane and effective organizations.

Berrett–Koehler
Publishers

A community dedicated to creating
a world that works for all

Dear Reader,

Thank you for picking up this book and joining our worldwide community
of Berrett-Koehler readers. We share ideas that bring positive change into
people's lives, organizations, and society.

To welcome you, we'd like to offer you a free e-book. You can pick from
among twelve of our bestselling books by entering the promotional code
BKP92E here: http://www.bkconnection.com/welcome.

When you claim your free e-book, we'll also send you a copy of our e-news-
letter, the *BK Communiqué*. Although you're free to unsubscribe, there are
many benefits to sticking around. In every issue of our newsletter you'll find

- A free e-book
- Tips from famous authors
- Discounts on spotlight titles
- Hilarious insider publishing news
- A chance to win a prize for answering a riddle

Best of all, our readers tell us, "Your newsletter is the only one I actually
read." So claim your gift today, and please stay in touch!

Sincerely,

Charlotte Ashlock
Steward of the BK Website

Questions? Comments? Contact me at bkcommunity@bkpub.com.